BUILDING RESILIENCE FOR SUCCESS

BUILDING RESILIENCE FOR SUCCESS

A Resource for Managers and Organizations

Cary L. Cooper

Professor of Organizational Psychology and Health,
Lancaster University, England

Jill Flint-Taylor

Director, Rusando Ltd, UK

and

Michael Pearn

Founder & CEO, Pearn Consulting LLC, San Francisco, US

palgrave
macmillan

First published 2013 by
PALGRAVE MACMILLAN

Palgrave Macmillan in the UK is an imprint of Macmillan Publishers Limited, registered in England, company number 785998, of Houndmills, Basingstoke, Hampshire RG21 6XS.

Palgrave Macmillan in the US is a division of St Martin's Press LLC, 175 Fifth Avenue, New York, NY 10010.

Palgrave Macmillan is the global academic imprint of the above companies and has companies and representatives throughout the world.

Palgrave® and Macmillan® are registered trademarks in the United States, the United Kingdom, Europe and other countries

ISBN: 978–0–230–36128–7

This book is printed on paper suitable for recycling and made from fully managed and sustained forest sources. Logging, pulping and manufacturing processes are expected to conform to the environmental regulations of the country of origin.

A catalogue record for this book is available from the British Library.

A catalog record for this book is available from the Library of Congress.

CONTENTS

LIST OF TABLES AND FIGURES

Tables

Figures

INTRODUCTION—SETTING THE SCENE

THE MEANING OF RESILIENCE AND THE PURPOSE OF OUR BOOK

The focus of this book is on building individual resilience—also known as psychological, emotional, or personal resilience. We use these terms interchangeably throughout, so what do we mean by them? The most straightforward, if somewhat narrow, answer is that this kind of resilience is being able to bounce back from setbacks and to stay effective in the face of tough demands and difficult circumstances. Expanding on this, our definition goes beyond recovery from stressful or potentially stressful events, to include the sustainability of that recovery and the lasting benefit—the strength that builds through coping well with such situations.[1] The capability that is developed in this way applies to coping with everyday problems and challenges—the need for individual resilience is by no means restricted to extreme circumstances or heroic acts.

Our purpose has been to put together a resource on which managers, human resource specialists, learning and development professionals, and others can draw to commission, design, deliver, and evaluate workplace resilience-building interventions. We describe and discuss many different approaches, findings, and practical applications and we share our own experiences, suggestions, and recommendations. It is not our intention to provide a prescriptive self-help guide or trainer's manual, but rather to offer a broad base of knowledge, ideas, and solutions that can be mined in various ways to meet different needs and organizational circumstances.

Firstly, in Part 1, we review developments in the field over the past twenty years or so, with reference to both research and practice. Based on this foundation of theory, evidence and experience we present a two-part framework that can be used to structure and facilitate resilience development within organizations. The style of Part 1 reflects an emphasis on applying expert knowledge from research and practice to develop a robust framework for use in organizations, and we provide detailed references for those who are interested in the science behind our approach.

Following this, in Part 2, we look further at the way practical resilience-building interventions have developed over the years in line with new research and theory, and we present detailed suggestions and examples to show what can be achieved in the organizational context. The style of this section reflects an emphasis on explaining different techniques and learning from the specific experiences of individuals and organizations. Key research references are provided where appropriate, but the main focus is on practical suggestions and examples.

Finally, in Part 3, we offer a strategic overview and further illustrations of some of the main ways in which resilience-building can be positioned within the context of wider organizational objectives and interventions, such as leadership development, organizational transformation, and performance enhancement.

COPING WITH PRESSURE—INDIVIDUAL DIFFERENCES

In referring to "individual" resilience we raise questions by highlighting the fact that this ability varies from one person to another. Many people have probably at one time or another watched a politician on television and doubted their own ability to remain as calm in the face of a storm of personal criticism. At other times they may be surprised by the vulnerability of a friend or colleague, recognizing that they have been less affected by similar circumstances. So it is important to know more about how this works—what is the nature of these personal differences; are they set in stone or can anyone improve their resilience over time?

As far as the last of these questions is concerned, this book is founded on the very good evidence that resilience can indeed be developed. More on this evidence shortly, and in later chapters we will explore a number of practical activities and approaches that can help to achieve this objective. To start with, however, we need to look in more detail at the fact that some people cope better than others, and why this is a matter for organizations as well as for those who work in them.

When we describe someone as resilient, we often mean that he or she copes well with pressure. We may even say they thrive on it. The opposite of this is generally referred to as "being vulnerable to stress, setbacks or disappointments." From this it becomes clear that pressure can be "positive" (challenging but energizing) or "negative" (stressful), so to understand resilience we need to understand the nature of pressure and stress.

The first point to make is that the same situation may be positively challenging for one person, but stressful for another. This could happen, for example, if a sales manager presents the quarterly results, and makes it clear that he or she is not happy with the team's performance. One member of the team may feel determined to try harder the following week, while another may feel anxious and discouraged. Another complication is that the same person may react quite differently from one week to the next, even if the message from the sales manager is very similar on both occasions.

There are many reasons for these different reactions, involving both situational factors and more intrinsic personal factors. Some of these influences may be obvious to the manager, or at least to the team member concerned. Other influences may be harder to pin down, but they nevertheless affect how each person feels as well as what he or she does next. Richard Lazarus[2] explained individual differences in the experience and expression of emotion in terms of a process he called "appraisal", commenting that:

> If two individuals appraise the same situation differently, their emotional responses will differ. And if they appraise different situations in the same way, their emotional response will be the same. Even *coping*...works by influencing and changing how the individual appraises the significance of what is happening and how it might be dealt with. (p. 336)

This theoretical position is just one of many that emphasize the role of perception and belief in determining how we react to events. In this, it is entirely consistent with our definition of stress, as arising when pressure exceeds your perceived ability to cope.[3] Richard Lazarus was talking about emotions in general, but many researchers and practicing psychologists have taken a similar view when focusing specifically on anxiety, depression, and stress. It is from this field of clinical psychology and mental health, including the study of

3

workplace stress, that much of our understanding of resilience has emerged.

It was, indeed, fortunate that during a long period when it was unfashionable in mainstream academic psychology to study emotions, an active interest in the causes and treatment of anxiety and depression ensured that knowledge of these issues continued to develop. However, the current, growing interest in resilience as a feature of the normal, adult life-cycle—outside the field of clinical psychology and mental ill-health—is a more recent development. We conclude at the end of this book that resilience, especially in organizational settings, has transitioned from a remedy for weakness to capacity builder to help the strong become stronger. Nonetheless, it is important to understand where the concept arose and why the need for it still has somewhat negative ring.

The normalization of resilience—the acceptance that it is a part of everyday life and work for everyone—comes at a time of rapidly growing interest in positive psychology. There is no doubt that the recent study of "positive emotions and experiences" has played an important role in emphasizing the potentially beneficial strength-building nature of "positive (or challenge) pressure." In addition, it has broadened our understanding of the range of ways in which resilience can be developed.

AN INTRODUCTION TO RESILIENCE-BUILDING IN THE WORKPLACE

One of the first contexts in which the more general interest in resilience became apparent was that of the workplace. In the 1970s and '80s, researchers in the United States began to investigate the qualities that helped some managers to cope more effectively with prolonged stressful circumstances than others.[4] In the late 1980s, the American psychologist Martin Seligman, who had been involved in anxiety and depression research for many years, began to take an interest in how the findings could be applied to helping employees cope with challenging work situations. He developed a one-day resilience training course for insurance sales representatives, whose job involved cold calling (making unsolicited marketing calls to potential customers) and a high level of rejection.

The success of Seligman's training inspired researchers at London's Institute of Psychiatry to develop a longer and more in-depth course, which they tested in the insurance industry and also with professionals and managers who had been continuously unemployed for more than a year. Again the results were very encouraging, with outcomes ranging from improved resilience and general well-being to higher sales and retention (in the insurance industry study), and a higher number of job interviews and job offers (among the unemployed participants) when compared with a control group who received different but relevant training.[5]

These resilience-building courses were acknowledged as practical and effective, and the design was implemented within a number of corporate and government programs. There were, however, several barriers to the wider spread of the approach, even within organizations that had already benefitted financially and in other ways through their participation in the research. To those of us involved in promoting the training in the corporate sector in the 1990s, it became clear that the main obstacle was a lack of industry-wide organizational readiness.[6]

This was indeed a problem, as "organizational readiness" is now known to be one of the main prerequisites for the successful implementation of innovative training and development programs. In terms of winning the "hearts and minds" of budget holders and senior stakeholders, the sales figures and cost savings made a strong, rational argument for rolling out the resilience training. Yet there was a more emotional distrust of any training with a "psychological" foundation, and anxiety about engaging with an issue so closely associated with workplace stress. "Resilience training" carried a bit of a stigma. It seemed to be intended for those who were failing to cope, and this perception has impeded the take-up of resilience development in organizations despite the solid evidence of financial and other benefits. Related to these concerns, some people have a skeptical view of resilience-building programs as a manipulative "management trick", designed to ensure that ever-increasing pressure can be applied to the workforce in the interests of maximizing output and profit.

While such reservations are still in evidence, they are under challenge from a growing conviction that coping with pressure is a critical skill in today's workplace. Acceptance has also been boosted by a shift away from remedial resilience training towards a "strengths-based" approach that has its roots in the increasingly popular Positive Psychology movement. In addition, recent research and practice have demonstrated a strong and direct relationship between individual well-being and organizational outcomes (including productivity). There is always a risk of any tool or method being used for cynical or exploitative purposes, but the expanding workplace well-being agenda helps to ensure that such interventions benefit both the individual and the organization.

Chapter 3 tells in more detail the story of how resilience development has found a place in organizations over the past twenty years, with momentum building up to the point where today it is widely seen as "an idea whose time has come." As a result, forward-thinking leadership teams are now actively seeking suitable resilience development solutions for all organization members or groups who are in critical roles or who are subject to more extreme pressures. We are even seeing a greater recognition of the need for this kind of support among the senior executives themselves, although for many this is still a difficult admission to make.

A TALE OF TWO CHIEF EXECUTIVES

When it comes to the pressures of leadership, there is no doubt that any chief executive can expect to face challenges that seem insurmountable at times. Just to get to that position in the first place requires a high level of personal resilience, but that is not the same thing as being invulnerable. More than one CEO has told us that appointment to the role presented the steepest—and loneliest—learning curve he or she had ever faced.

So consider the following stories. The first is of the founder of one of the world's most successful hi-tech companies, who thrived on pressures the rest of us could hardly imagine only to succumb to what is widely considered to have been a treatable cancer. When asked why treatment had been delayed, Steve Jobs' biographer is quoted as saying, "I think he kind of felt: if you ignore something you don't want to exist, you can have magical thinking. It had worked for him in the past. He'd regret it."[7]

Our second tale is that of the CEO of the UK's largest retail bank, who took an extended period of sick leave after "suffering fatigue due to over-work" yet about whom "colleagues say he is obsessive about detail, but is cool under pressure and shows few signs of stress."[8]

Of course we can never know the full truth of what went wrong in either case. However, just these short accounts make it clear that personal resilience is not a simple matter, that even the strongest have their Achilles' heel, and that there is always a risk of being undermined by the very qualities and beliefs that have been the foundation of our success for many years.

Reflecting on these stories gives us five core principles:

1. Individuals vary in both the nature and degree of their ability to cope with pressures and setbacks.
2. Psychological resilience is complex rather than one-dimensional. It is not something we either have or lack altogether—most of us are resilient in some ways, but less so in others.
3. Even the most resilient people have their limits, although they may be less alert to when these limits are being reached.
4. Certain qualities and beliefs, such as optimism or self-confidence, may boost our resilience in most situations but can harm it if they are taken to extremes.
5. Resilience results from the interaction of an individual and their situation—it is not a fixed personality trait and it can be developed.

OVERVIEW OF THE BOOK

Throughout this book we aim to provide a framework that facilitates the integration of personal resilience development interventions with broad, strategic programs to improve individual well-being and organizational performance. Integral to our approach is the need to factor in an understanding of the work context—in particular an understanding of the main sources of workplace pressure and support. Without this understanding it is difficult to make the most of opportunities to develop resilience on the job, yet this is a context that can produce far greater improvements than the widely used format of a short, one-off training session.

Part 1

Understanding resilience

Chapter 1 addresses the question of individual differences, and sets out a framework for understanding personal resilience strengths and risks. This includes a more detailed definition of resilience, as well as a review of the relevant research and information on a variety of diagnostic tools and approaches.

In Chapter 2 we look at the individual in the workplace. We describe the main sources of workplace pressure and support, and discuss how these are likely to affect individuals differently, depending on the nature and level of their personal resilience. The focus here is on the interaction between a person and his or her work situation, and the way in which an individual's resilience resources may be boosted or undermined by this interaction.

Chapter 3 tells the story "from then to now", for those who have a professional interest in understanding the background to where we are today and who want to make sure resilience development is not just a passing fad in their organization.

Part 2

Building resilience

Chapters 4 and 5 look at what individuals can do to build their resilience, both on their own and with the support of their employers. The emphasis here is on resilience-building as a personal quest and a "whole-life" endeavor—even if the catalyst and support are provided by the work context. Chapter 4 focuses on understanding your personal starting point and making use of two major resilience-building techniques that have a broad application for a wide range of needs and contexts. Chapter 5 addresses more specifically how to raise personal resilience within the framework of the four main components of resilience (introduced in Chapter 1).

In Chapters 6 and 7 we focus on approaches managers and employing organizations can take to support resilience-building. This is divided into resilience-focused interventions, such as coaching and resilience workshops (Chapter 6), and good management practices and strategies that are particularly relevant to developing resilience (Chapter 7). We make a clear distinction between improving the resilience of individuals, and raising levels of well-being in the team (a more temporary collective state we refer to as "team resilience").

Part 3

Resilience-building for future success

Chapter 8 takes an overview of implications for employers, with further real-life illustrations of the different forms that team and organizational interventions might take.

Appendices

Appendix I is a short guide to using this book as a resource for developing your own interventions. In Appendix II we offer guidelines on creating a personal resilience plan, and in Appendix III we offer a detailed list of topics that can be included in resilience training and development.

Finally, by way of introduction, we need to be clear about what will *not* be covered in this book. In focusing on individual or personal resilience, we do not address in any detail the question of group or organizational resilience. Organizational resilience is much more than the sum of the personal resilience of employees, managers, and leaders—it includes such diverse capabilities as disaster relief planning for technology systems and long-term financial planning. Similarly, the resilience of departments and teams is a collective characteristic of the group and depends on a wide range of factors such as adequate resourcing, effective communication channels, efficient structures, and a constructive management style.

We do touch briefly on what we refer to as "team resilience", a kind of group resilience achieved when high levels of well-being increase the team's ability to bounce back and keep going in the face of tough challenges. Team resilience is a product of the effective management of the sources of workplace pressure and support (described in Chapter 2), which also have an important impact on individual resilience. The two are, however, quite distinct and any detailed discussion of team resilience is outside the scope of this book.

PART 1

UNDERSTANDING RESILIENCE

CHAPTER 1

"THE INDIVIDUAL"— A FRAMEWORK FOR UNDERSTANDING PERSONAL RESILIENCE

RESILIENCE RISKS AND STRENGTHS—FROM RISK MANAGEMENT TO CAPACITY-BUILDING

To understand individual differences in resilience, we need to move beyond the working definition set out in the Introduction, and look at some of the other ways this complex concept has been defined and researched. Traditionally, resilience has been studied from the angle of providing therapeutic support for people who are experiencing difficulty in coping with crisis, bereavement, or life in general. In seeking to understand why some people cope better than others, much of this work has focused on the development of resilience in childhood and adolescence.

Lately, more attention has been paid to studying resilience in adulthood, and also to resilience-building as an asset or strength, rather than as a solution to a crisis or problem. Evidence is also mounting for the view that resilience may even be the norm and that people in general are more resilient than earlier studies may have indicated. George Bonanno suggests that resilience, rather than collapse and recovery, is the most common outcome from traumatic events.[1] He also makes the useful and important distinction between resilience in coping with long-term problems or "corrosive" environments on the one hand, and resilience to isolated events on the other.

These more recent lines of investigation are particularly relevant to our aim of integrating resilience-building with broader programs to improve employee well-being and business performance, because

13

they help to normalize the idea of resilience development and take it outside the "white coat" context of illness, therapy, and crisis management.

THE CHALLENGE OF DEFINING RESILIENCE

One thing everyone agrees on is the lack of a common definition of resilience. Indeed, it is not unusual to read several different definitions within the same book or article (such as the handbook by John Reich and his colleagues; see box[2]).

Definitions and descriptions of personal resilience from contributors to the *Handbook of Adult Resilience* (2010)

"...resilience is best defined as an outcome of successful adaptation to adversity. Characteristics of the person and situation may identify resilient processes, but only if they lead to healthier outcomes following stressful circumstances." (Zautra and others, p. 4)

"Resilience has numerous meanings in prior research, but generally refers to a pattern of functioning indicative of 'positive adaptation' in the context of 'risk' or adversity." (Ong and others p. 82)

"Resilience is a term psychologists use to refer to people's ability to cope with and find meaning in...stressful life events, in which individuals must respond with healthy intellectual functioning and supportive social relationships (Richardson, 2002)." (Mayer and Faber, p. 95)

"Resilience refers to individual differences or life experiences that help people to cope positively with adversity, make them better able to deal with stress in the future, and confer protection from the development of mental disorders under stress (Richardson, 2002)." (Skodol p. 113)

"Resilience is a broad concept that generally refers to positive adaptation in any kind of dynamic system that comes under challenge or threat." (Masten and Obradović, 2008)

"*Human resilience* refers to the processes or patterns of positive adaptation and development in the context of significant threats to an individual's life or function." (Masten and Wright, p. 215)

There is even debate about whether resilience should be seen as an outcome, a process, or a set of characteristics, and this divergence of opinion is reflected in some of the common measures of resilience. Some researchers use the term "resilience" to differentiate the "process" from the "personal characteristics," which they call "resiliency." Others, however, use only one of these terms, or use both interchangeably.

Other influential definitions follow:

- Resilience is "the phenomenon that some individuals have a relatively good outcome despite suffering risk experiences that would be expected to bring about serious sequelae."[3]
- "The construct of resilience refers to the ability of individuals to adapt successfully in the face of acute stress, trauma, or chronic adversity, maintaining or rapidly regaining psychological well-being and physiological homeostasis."[4]
- "Psychological resilience refers to effective coping and adaptation although faced with loss, hardship, or adversity."[5]
- "Resilience is the process of negotiating, managing and adapting to significant sources of stress or trauma."[6]

The multiplicity of definitions can be confusing and lacking in rigor from an academic point of view, but for practitioners they can also help to provide a richer understanding of the diverse perspectives and insights in the field. As psychologists Christopher Peterson and Martin Seligman suggest in their book on character strengths and virtues, resilience is not a unitary construct and is probably best seen as an umbrella term.[7] This is how we have chosen to use the term "resilience" throughout the book—in other words, we do not restrict its use to any specific academic construct.

Our umbrella view is reflected in the broad, working definition we presented in the Introduction: *resilience is being able to bounce back from setbacks and to keep going in the face of tough demands and difficult circumstances, including the enduring strength that builds from coping well with challenging or stressful events*. Our description deliberately emphasizes the process and outcome aspects of resilience. We see personality and other individual characteristics, along with external circumstances and events, as the predictive factors that explain why some people display better coping and more resilient outcomes than others. Our view on individual characteristics as the factors that underpin resilience is developed throughout this chapter.

15

The "four waves" of resilience research

In summarizing the academic research on resilience, Ann Masten and Margaret Wright[8] refer to "four waves of resilience research." The *first wave* focused on describing, defining, and measuring resilience, and produced highly consistent findings in terms of the characteristics of individuals, relationships, and resources that predicted resilience (if not in terms of how resilience should be defined!). The *second wave* looked at the processes through which resilience develops, with the *third wave* seeking to apply an understanding of these processes to design resilience-building interventions.

The *fourth wave* combines the insights and methods of different fields including psychology, genetics, neurobehavioral development, and statistics. It also, as noted above, focuses more than previously on the positive, strength-building aspects of resilience. For the organizational practitioner, such an approach is very welcome as it facilitates the promotion of resilience development in a context where remedial interventions tend to be treated with suspicion or relegated to the domain of occupational health.

What, then, do we know about the predictors of resilience? From the study of resilience in childhood, the following have emerged as the critical factors: *relationships* (particularly early parent–child relationships), *individual capabilities* (including problem-solving ability, self-motivation, self-control, and optimism/positive belief), and *cultural influences*. Cultural influence refers to the potentially protective role of cultural or religious beliefs and practices. For example, despite a range of socioeconomic and other pressures affecting Hispanics living in the United States, physical health outcomes for this group are often equal to or better than non-Hispanic Caucasian Americans.[9] This is an important reminder to take cultural differences into account when planning and implementing a resilience-building intervention in the workplace.

Missing in the research literature, however, according to Christopher Peterson and Martin Seligman, "is any discussion about which protective factors are relevant for whom, under what stressful circumstances, and with respect to what desirable outcomes."[10] They suggest that any such connections are likely to be general rather than highly specific, but the important point in our view is that more account should be taken of contextual factors when seeking to help people evaluate and improve their personal resilience.

16

This is an issue we seek to address in our approach to resilience at work—through reference to a research-based framework of the main sources of workplace pressure and support.[11] Given the multi-dimensional nature of resilience, there is no doubt that different work pressures will affect each of us in different ways—based not only on our current situation but also on the network of protective factors that has set the foundation for our personal resilience. In any event, participants in a resilience development program are more likely to engage with and benefit from an evaluation of their own particular resilience strengths and risks if this analysis is set in the context of the typical challenges and pressures they are likely to face in the work environment.

RESILIENCE—INDIVIDUAL CHARACTERISTICS

The framework we use for understanding the sources of workplace pressure and support ("the Situation") is described in the next chapter. Looking first at "the Individual" side of the equation, we turn to the question of what personal characteristics underpin or predict resilience. Table 1.1 gives an indication of the range of findings and perspectives on this issue. The conclusions presented in the table are drawn from studies that cover resilience development in childhood and adolescence, adult resilience, the genetic and biological determinants of resilience, sports performance, physical health, therapy and counseling, the management of organizational change, and other related topics.

In this book on individual resilience in the workplace, we do not go into detail on the biological, environmental, familial, or cultural factors that interact during childhood and adolescence to determine whether individuals demonstrate high or low levels of resilience in responding to the challenges of their work situation. Our focus is on helping to evaluate and develop the particular strengths that each person brings as an adult to the work situation, as well as the risks that each needs to manage in order to respond in a resilient way to pressures from work and home. For this we need to understand the interplay between the personal characteristics of employees, the main sources of workplace pressure and support, and the processes by which resilient outcomes are achieved (see Figure 1.1). This interplay is often referred to in the study of psychology as the interaction between the individual and the situation, and to help explore how it

Table 1.1 *Examples of individual characteristics found to be associated with resilience*

Author/researcher	Characteristics associated with resilience	Reference
Diane Coutu	Capacity to accept and confront reality Ability to find meaning in life Ability to improvise	"How Resilience Works," in *Harvard Business Review* on Building Personal and Organizational Resilience[12]
Salvatore Maddi and Deborah Khoshaba	Hardiness—a pattern of attitude and skills Resilient attitudes: commitment, control, and challenge (the 3Cs) Vital skills: transformational coping (to solve problems), interacting with others (to deepen social support)	*Resilience at Work: How to Succeed No Matter What Life Throws at You*[13]
Dennis Charney	Developing resilience in childhood and adolescence—key factors from the research: "good intellectual functioning, effective self-regulation of emotions and attachment behaviors, a positive self-concept, optimism, altruism, a capacity to convert traumatic helplessness into learned helpfulness, and an active coping style in confronting a stressor." From adult studies (largely in military situations): "an ability to bond with a group with a common mission, a high value placed on altruism, and the capacity to tolerate high levels of fear and still perform effectively."	*Psychobiological Mechanisms of Resilience and Vulnerability: Implications for Successful Adaptation to Extreme Stress*[14]

Timothy Smith	Resilience to health risks (physical): Negative factors: chronic anger/hostility; neuroticism/negative affectivity e.g. anxiety or sadness; a socially dominant style Positive factors: optimism, conscientiousness	"Personality as Risk and Resilience in Physical Health"[15]
Anthony Mancini and George Bonanno	Resilience in the face of bereavement: Self-enhancing biases, attachment style, repressive coping, a priori beliefs, identity continuity and complexity, and positive emotions	"Predictors and Parameters of Resilience to Loss: Toward an Individual Differences Model"[16]
Andrew Skodol	Resilient personalities: Sense of self (strong, well-differentiated and integrated), including self-esteem, self-confidence/self-efficacy, self-understanding, and self-control Interpersonal skills: sociability, emotional expressiveness, and interpersonal understanding	From the *Handbook of Adult Resilience*[17]

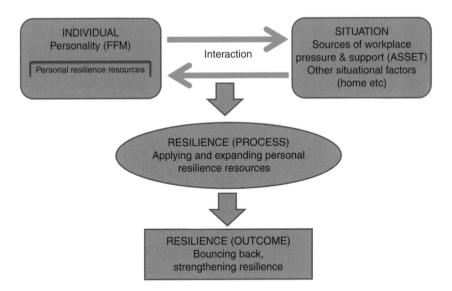

FIGURE 1.1   **Framework for understanding employees' resilience to workplace pressures**

works we need a framework for describing the individual and one for describing the situation.

As mentioned earlier, our framework for the work situation is a well-established and validated model of the main sources of work-place pressure and support (see next chapter). For the individual, we use the Five-Factor Model (FFM) of personality,[18] with reference, as appropriate, to other constructs such as reasoning ability. In giving particular emphasis to personality we agree with John Mayer and Michael Faber's view of personality as "the individual's master psychological system [which] oversees and organizes mental subsystems, such as motives, thoughts and self-control."[19] This system is the product of the interaction of biological, environmental, and other factors during childhood and adolescence.

We use the FFM to help us make the links between the individual and the work situation, because it is widely recognized as the most robust and well-researched description of the structure of adult personality,[20] and because we and others have spent many years researching the connections between FFM traits on the one hand,

and work-related outcomes (including performance and well-being) on the other.[21]

Why the FFM?

The Five-Factor Model of personality emerged into the mainstream of personality research in 1991, with the publication of two influential studies.[22],[23] Both:

- were "meta-analytic" studies, that is, they pulled together and analyzed the findings of many smaller studies using a wide variety of personality measures;
- made direct reference to the validity of personality traits for the prediction of work performance;
- used the FFM as the over-arching framework to combine the different personality models used by the smaller studies;
- came up with powerful findings in support of the relationships between personality and work performance.

These researchers used the FFM because it was beginning to achieve greater consensus among experts than the field had ever seen before, in terms of the number of personality factors (clusters of traits) and the best way of describing and measuring personality. Even firm supporters of the 16PF,[24] the Myers-Briggs,[25] and the OPQ[26] quickly recognized the case for mapping these instruments on to the five-factor structure in a series of studies and articles. As a result, during the 1990s, research using the FFM revolutionized the potential of personality assessment for the prediction and development of competency-based performance and other work-related outcomes.

To a large extent, however, this potential has remained unrealized in the practical arena of work-based selection and assessment. There are a number of likely reasons for this, including the stronghold that certain commercial measures of personality already had, and have maintained, on the market. Also, much of the power of the FFM lies in the detail (as in the 36 facet scales of its best-established questionnaire, the NEO PI-R), while the most popular measures for use in the workplace are those that present very simple and intuitive summary profiles. Gradually, however, use of the FFM is beginning to spread, aided by well-informed practitioners and a few expert system reports that make the detail more accessible and intuitive.[27]

A warning: the labels typically given to the scales (see Figure 1.2) give a strong impression that it is "better" to be at one end of the scale than at the other, e.g. to be emotionally stable rather than neurotic. Looking beyond the labels, however, it turns out that there are dangers at each end of the scale. For example, people who are very low on *Neuroticism* may put themselves and others at risk by underestimating problems, while people who are very high on *Conscientiousness* can be inflexible. Evidence suggests the variation in our personalities has an evolutionary benefit—anxiety can be very good for survival in some situations, as can conservatism, introversion etc.

Typically, researchers have sought to identify a limited number of specific personality characteristics that mark out the most resilient people—rather than starting with a comprehensive model of personality such as the FFM and seeking to understand the different ways in which each trait or combinations of traits may relate to resilience in different situations. The "resilient personality" approach can be illustrated by the model of psychological hardiness, one of the few developed with a specific focus on the work context.

Psychological hardiness

Some of the researchers mentioned in Table 1.1 have included personal characteristics as one element of their investigation of resilience. Others have focused their attention specifically on identifying these individual differences. For example, in 1979, Suzanne Kobasa[28] reported her findings on the protective function performed by a set of personality characteristics she labeled "hardiness." Her study involved comparing a group of managers and executives who suffered ill-health due to stress with a second group who remained healthy under similar pressures. Those who remained healthy under pressure were found to have higher levels of the "3Cs": the dispositions of Commitment, Control, and Challenge. *Commitment* refers to engaging with one's environment and having a sense of purpose or meaning. *Control* refers to feeling able to influence events (sometimes described as an internal locus of control). *Challenge* refers to seeing change as normal and welcome—an opportunity rather than a threat.

This work was part of a long and enduring research tradition involving a number of influential psychologists including Salvatore Maddi, who

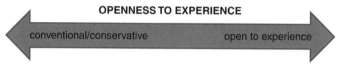

OPENNESS TO EXPERIENCE

conventional/conservative   open to experience

Specific traits:
Imagination, Aesthetic appreciation, Openness to emotional experience, Openness to new activities and approaches, Intellectual curiosity, Openness to different values

CONSCIENTIOUSNESS

careless, unstructured   conscientious

Specific traits:
Sense of competence, Liking for order, Sense of duty, Desire to achieve, Self-Discipline, Deliberation

EXTRAVERSION

introverted   extraverted

Specific traits:
Warmth, Sociability, Assertiveness, Activity/energy, Excitement seeking, Positive emotions

AGREEABLENESS

egocentric, sceptical   altruistic, supportive

Specific traits:
Willingness to trust others, Straightforwardness/directness, Altruism, Compliance/tolerance, Modesty, Tender-mindedness/sympathy

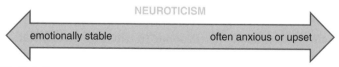

NEUROTICISM

emotionally stable   often anxious or upset

Specific traits:
Anxiety, Angry hostility, Depression, Self-Consciousness, Impulsiveness (low self-control), Vulnerability to stress

FIGURE 1.2 **Overview of the "OCEAN" Five-Factor Model (FFM) of personality**

Note: Specific traits derived from the NEO PI-R questionnaire and similar frameworks.

went on to found the Hardiness Institute in California, and Mihaly Csikszentmihalyi, now a central figure in the positive psychology movement. Further research focusing specifically on the hardiness concept included a large-scale study of supervisors and managers at the Illinois Bell Telephone company over a twelve-year period (1975–1986) of considerable organizational change. Salvatore Maddi and Deborah Khoshaba describe the findings and practical implications in their book, *Resilience at Work: How to Succeed No Matter What Life Throws at You.*[29]

Interestingly, in this later formulation of hardiness, the "3Cs" are presented as "resilient attitudes" rather than dispositions, and are seen as being complemented by the "two vital skills" of transformational coping (transforming potentially stressful changes to your advantage) and social support (interacting with others in a constructive way that builds and preserves relationships). This change is consistent with our view of resilience as process and outcome, underpinned or predicted by more enduring personality traits and other personal characteristics—as opposed to resilience being a trait or set of traits.

Mental toughness in sport

While much of the work on hardiness was done in the context of supervision and management in organizations, a related concept labeled "mental toughness" has gained currency in the world of sport. Perhaps unsurprisingly, given the intuitive appeal of the label, mental toughness has come to mean many different things to different practitioners. This situation is not helped by what some see as a lack of clarity and rigor in research on the topic.[30] In one of the more robust approaches, Peter Clough and Keith Earle[31] drew directly on the hardiness research and their own work with rugby league players to put forward a "4Cs" model of mental toughness and to develop the MTQ48 (Mental Toughness Questionnaire 48). The fourth "C" in this measure is *Confidence* (confidence in interpersonal situations and confidence in one's own abilities). Recent studies have investigated the relationship between mental toughness and various qualities considered to be important for resilience. In one such study, mental toughness was found to be related to optimism and the ability to cope with pressure, and specifically with a tendency to tackle issues and problems directly rather than using avoidance strategies to cope.[32]

PERSONAL CHARACTERISTICS THAT UNDERPIN RESILIENCE: COMMON THEMES

There are many other theories and approaches to the study of individual differences in coping with pressure, some of which we refer to in later chapters as we discuss the design and implementation of resilience-building approaches in the work context. There are, however, some clear commonalities and themes emerging, and this is what we focus on now.

Intelligence and problem solving

It has been known for some time that the relationship between anxiety, stress, and work performance is a complex one. Anxiety and stress are clearly related, and high levels of stress are known to have a negative effect on work performance. Yet the personality trait of anxiety (being a typically anxious person) does not appear to have as much of a negative effect on performance as might be expected. It turns out that this is because other factors come into play and determine the extent to which anxiety has a detrimental effect—and one of these factors is intelligence (reasoning or cognitive ability). Quite simply, it helps to have the intellectual ability to assess a situation, identify solutions, evaluate options, and work out a plan. People with good "problem-solving" abilities may still feel anxious, but they have a better chance of figuring out a solution—their intellectual ability acts as a protective factor against stress and poor performance. In these circumstances, a certain amount of anxiety may also make a positive contribution to resilience, by ensuring that problems are recognized and dealt with.

This does not mean, however, that the most resilient people are those with the highest levels of intelligence—it is more a question of being able to develop a sound understanding of your situation, and to evaluate how it is likely to develop and what options are open to you. There is, however, some evidence to suggest that people with higher levels of intelligence may be more susceptible than their peers to certain kinds of pressure.[33]

These days, "reasoning ability" is no longer seen as the only kind of intelligence. The psychologist and author, Daniel Goleman, is well known for popularizing the idea of emotional intelligence: "emotional intelligence is observed when a person demonstrates the competencies that constitute self-awareness, self-management, social awareness, and social skills at appropriate times and ways in sufficient frequency to be effective in the situation."[34] Before this, others referred to social/interpersonal intelligence, intrapersonal/personal intelligence, and practical intelligence. These constructs are sometimes referred to collectively as "hot intelligence," in reference to the fact that they are closely associated with emotion and to distinguish them from the kind of "cold," logical intelligence measured by standard tests of reasoning ability or "IQ." The "hot" forms of intelligence have an important role to play in resilience, and we deal with them separately in the following sections.

Self-control

Sometimes referred to as self-management or self-regulation, self-control involves the ability to manage your emotions and behavior in an adaptive way that delivers a good outcome for you and those around you. It is the product of a number of factors that differ from one person to another, such as being able to pay selective attention to certain aspects of your environment and being able to delay gratification—giving up your favorite biscuits so that you can fit into your shorts on holiday, for example!

As with all personal characteristics, self-control is known to result from the interaction of a number of biological, environmental, and social factors. The link with childhood upbringing is obvious—the development of their children's ability to manage emotions and behavior is clearly something that most parents invest considerable energy in. The process and implications of developing self-control have been a major focus of psychologists and psychiatrists in the psychoanalytic tradition (following the theories of Sigmund Freud, Carl Jung, and their colleagues).

In the most widely used version of the Five-Factor Model of personality, or FFM (see Figure 1.2), a scale labeled "impulsiveness" is included within the *Neuroticism* cluster of traits—with high levels of impulsiveness being equated to low levels of self-control. Unsurprisingly, *Neuroticism* (the opposite pole of which is generally labeled *Emotional Stability*) is widely associated with a lack of resilience.

Adults with poor self-control have a tendency to give in to their impulses, despite an inner voice warning them against what they are about to say or do. There are a number of reasons why this has a negative effect on their resilience, including potential damage to self-esteem and to the relationships with friends and family that are an important source of support in hard times.

Self-awareness

As can be seen from this observation on self-control, self-esteem, and relationships, the links among the various resilience-related characteristics and skills are many and complex. It is hard to imagine someone managing their emotions and behavior effectively without a good level of self-awareness. People who understand why they may be feeling in a certain way, and who can predict how they are likely to respond in different circumstances, are in a more informed position when deciding what to do next. They may, however, still decide to ignore their inner voice and go with their impulses—it is quite possible to have good self-awareness but poor self-control.

Self-awareness is also closely linked to the development and maintenance of supportive relationships. People with poor self-awareness may, for example, find that they upset others without recognizing that this is likely to happen—not from any bad intention, but because they are not in touch with their own attitudes, assumptions, or feelings. To illustrate, someone who is more angry than he or she realizes may speak in a tone of voice that conveys the full weight of that anger, even though the intention is to deal with the situation rationally and constructively.

Awareness of others/empathy

The complementary skill to self-awareness is "other-awareness"—being quick to pick up on how other people are feeling from what they say and do, and drawing accurate conclusions from this about what they are thinking. This information about the thoughts, beliefs, and intentions of those you work with is invaluable in so many ways. It can be used to motivate teams, to build strong relationships, and to achieve success in the toughest negotiations. Without it you would be operating in the dark as you try to steer through the potential minefield of work relationships.

Awareness of others is often referred to as "empathy"—the ability to put yourself in someone else's shoes and appreciate how he or she is feeling. Empathy implies more than simply recognizing emotions in someone else—it includes experiencing a certain level of the same emotion yourself. It is linked to but conceptually distinct from sympathy, which is a supportive response to someone else's difficulties or distress. It is possible to take a sympathetic view of someone's situation without experiencing any of the same emotions as they do. Equally, it is possible to have no sympathy for someone's situation—for example when they are trying to negotiate a higher rate than you believe is reasonable—while having a very good appreciation of how they are feeling (empathy) and why they have decided to take that position.

Understanding accurately why someone has taken a certain decision is not, however, a necessary outcome from appreciating how they are feeling. Recognizing their emotions provides you with some good evidence on which to base your hypotheses about their past actions and future responses, but these are still only hypotheses. Even if you are entirely accurate about the emotions someone is experiencing, you still do not know what they are thinking. They may be frustrated with you for being slow to respond, or they may be frustrated with themselves for not knowing the answer to the question. Just knowing that they are feeling frustrated does not tell you all you need to know about how to react to the situation—it does not even tell you a great deal about how they see it.

Full awareness of others means appreciating how they are feeling and drawing sound, unbiased conclusions as to the attitudes, thoughts, and beliefs that are driving these emotions. As a protective factor for resilience, it is the first building block in developing, maintaining, and managing constructive, supportive work relationships. It is also (as in a situation of tough negotiation) one of the essential skills you need to protect yourself from the harmful intentions of other people and to achieve successful outcomes in challenging circumstances for yourself, your team, and your customers, clients or stakeholders.

In terms of the FFM, awareness of others and self-awareness are both most closely related to the specific trait of *Openness to Emotional Experience*. The relationship is not, however, as simple and direct as in the case of self-control. It is likely, for example, that a sociable interest in other people is also an important factor in awareness of others.

Sociability

Sociability and the related characteristic of *Warmth* have been identified by resilience researchers as important for resilience in their own right, beyond their role in helping to develop an aware-ness of other people. People who enjoy the company of others are more likely to reach out to build relationships and typically have more energy to sustain high levels of interaction. *Warmth* and *Sociability* are two specific traits within the *Extraversion* clus-ter of the FFM, and there are some who say that *Extraversion* as a whole is a positive predictor of resilient outcomes. This may be the case if *Extraversion* is measured as a single overall factor, but at the detailed level there is one aspect of *Extraversion* that shows a more complex relationship with resilience. This is the trait of *Dominance*, or *Assertiveness*. In Table 1.1, a socially domi-nant style is listed as a negative predictor of resilience in the context of physical health outcomes. It seems that being impa-tient and forceful carries certain risks for stress-related physical conditions, and it is quite likely that it has its downside in rela-tion to psychological resilience as well—for example through the impact an overly dominant style can have on relationships with colleagues.

Another individual characteristic, or set of characteristics, with a less straightforward relationship to resilience is the FFM factor of *Agreeableness* (a concerned and supportive approach to dealing with other people). Some writers on resilience have a tendency to put sociability and *Agreeableness* together, and at first sight this seems perfectly reasonable, as both are clearly important for building and maintaining good relationships. *Extraversion* and *Agreeableness* are, however, entirely distinct personality factors and it is quite possible for someone to have high levels of *Extraversion* and low levels of *Agreeableness*—a pattern sometimes described as being a "disagree-able extravert." Such people are outgoing and sociable but at the same time quite competitive and tough-minded in their attitudes towards others—and it may come as a surprise to realize they are less cuddly than you thought once you get to know them better!

Again, studies that have found high levels of *Agreeableness* to be associated with measures of resilience may well have overlooked some of the important detail. Being generally supportive of friends, family, and colleagues is certainly an important factor in building the support network you need for your own resilience. However, it is not difficult to imagine situations in which resilience is undermined by being naively trusting or afraid of standing your ground—both specific aspects of high *Agreeableness*.

This is where attempts to identify the "resilient personality" break down. Because resilience is multi-dimensional, the reality is that characteristics such as *Agreeableness* are likely to be positive for certain aspects—such as building supportive networks of relationships—but less positive for other aspects—such as withstanding unreasonable demands. In addition, even where a characteristic plays a protective role, an excess of that characteristic may have the opposite effect. So, for example, being willing to compromise is good for flexibility and relationships, but taken to extreme this becomes fear of conflict, which can undermine relationships through failure to address issues openly and promptly.

Conscientiousness

Another FFM factor that has been identified by resilience researchers as being associated with resilience is *Conscientiousness*. This cluster includes having a *Sense of Duty*, a liking for order and structure (*Order*), and good *Self-Discipline*. The desire to achieve is also usually seen as being part of *Conscientiousness*, although some models suggest that this is a separate factor. As with *Agreeableness*, the relationship with resilience appears to have been established largely by using a short, global measure of *Conscientiousness*. When we look at the detail, we see a similar pattern—being well organized because you have a need for order can be useful in pre-empting problems and coping with pressure. There is, however, no doubt that a high need for order can make it difficult to respond in an adaptable and flexible manner.

Adaptability/ability to improvise

The ability to adapt to changing circumstances is one of the most widely recognized resilience requirements of today's workforce. Clearly, those who find rapid and continuous change hard to manage are likely to be under increasing pressure as social, economic, and environmental uncertainties escalate and organizations struggle to reinvent themselves in order to survive. Intelligence, both hot and cold, is one determinant of our ability to adapt. In addition, studies linking other traits to competencies[35] have produced a number of interesting results.

Picking up on the point we have just made about *Conscientiousness*, there is evidence to suggest a positive relationship between moderately low scores on some *Conscientiousness* traits on the one hand, and the ability to think and respond flexibly, on the other. People who favor an unstructured approach—who like to keep things open rather than planning and organizing all the details in advance—have an advantage when it comes to responding in a flexible way and generating creative solutions, especially if they are also comfortable with thinking on their feet and acting without having all the facts at their disposal.

That is not to say that organized, structured people lack adaptability—planning can, of course, be very helpful in dealing with changing situations and demands. However, your personal resilience strengths and risks will be quite different in kind depending on whether you are a natural organizer or someone who prefers to take things as they come. Once again the key is recognizing the complex nature of resilience and the risks posed by any characteristics that are taken to extreme (over-used).

The FFM personality cluster most strongly associated with adaptability is that of *Openness to Experience*—especially the specific traits of *Imagination*, *Openness to New Activities and Approaches*, and *Intellectual Curiosity*. Of all the different personality factors, *Openness* is most closely related to intellectual abilities such as creativity and problem solving. In our research, we have found it to be one of the most important predictors of the leadership competency of strategic perspective—seeing the big picture and looking ahead to anticipate and respond to future business challenges and requirements.

Positive emotions

The idea that positive emotions are associated with resilience may seem too obvious to be worth mentioning. The interesting question, however, is the nature of this relationship. If resilience is seen as an outcome, then we might well expect people experiencing such an outcome to feel good about it. There is no doubt that coping successfully with tough challenges has this effect, but it seems that the reverse is also true—that experiencing positive emotions can play an instrumental role in helping one to respond in a resilient way in the first place.

Positive psychologists Michele Tugade and Barbara Fredrickson[36] were interested in the way resilient people appear actively to generate positive emotions when faced with potentially stressful circumstances. Evidence from a number of studies suggested that such people use a variety of strategies related to humor, relaxation, and optimistic thinking. Tugade and Fredrickson set out to find more about how the relationship between positive emotions and resilience works, using the broaden-and-build theory of positive emotions. This theory suggests that a person's range of thoughts and actions is broadened by experiencing positive emotions—a result that strengthens their personal resources.

Their studies have provided evidence for the idea that the generation of positive emotions is a coping strategy in its own right, and not simply the result of coping with a situation in a resilient way. Some of this evidence came from research on reactions to the September 11, 2001 attacks in the United States—a study that looked specifically at resilience, positive affect (positive emotions), and the FFM. The results indicated that low levels of *Neuroticism*, high levels of *Extraversion*, and high levels of *Openness to Experience* all led to positive affect, and were all associated with resilient outcomes.[37]

Other evidence suggests that these personality traits—*Neuroticism* and *Extraversion* in particular—are at least partly "hard-wired," or rooted in biological predispositions. Definitely it is well established that every individual falls somewhere along a continuum on each— between introversion and extraversion, for example. The implication is, therefore, that people have a head start when it comes to generating the positive emotions that protect them from stress and enable them to bounce back from setbacks.

Positive attitudes and beliefs

To understand how positive emotions can be within the control of the person concerned, we need to look at an aspect of resilience that is probably more important than any other for the design of workplace resilience-building interventions. This is the power of someone's thoughts, attitudes, and beliefs—the way they drive how that person feels and behaves. When something good or bad happens to someone, they often notice how they feel before they recognize what they think or believe about it. In many cases they never really bottom out what those thoughts and beliefs are, even when the emotions they experience are very strong. Yet many years ago it was proven that the sequence of events is always as follows: thoughts first, then feelings and actions. As illustrated in Figure 1.3, something happens (Activating event) and how you feel and behave (Consequence) depends on what you believe to be true (Belief)—how you see the situation, how you interpret your own and others' part in it, what you think is likely to happen next, and so on.[38]

The reason people often experience the emotion first is because some of their most powerful reactions are driven by "automatic" thoughts—fleeting thoughts that come from deeply held beliefs and assumptions they are hardly aware of much of the time, if at all. So, for example, if your boss asks you to come and see her the following day and you immediately feel very anxious, you may have already been told by a colleague that she intends to give you bad news, or you may know nothing about her intentions but be assuming the worst. Of course when you have little evidence you need to make an assumption about what is going on. The problem comes when these assumptions are driven by deeply held (and often inaccessible) but inaccurate beliefs—about one's own vulnerability or lack of competence, for example.

This knowledge about how thoughts drive emotions is important for workplace resilience development because of the success that has been achieved through training people to "catch" their fleeting, automatic thoughts and subject them to scrutiny—challenging those deeply held assumptions and beliefs that do not stand up to the evidence once they are exposed to the light of day, and learning to replace them with equally believable but more helpful and accurate alternatives. The techniques used in this training are derived from Cognitive–Behavioural Therapy—an approach that focuses on thoughts and behaviors to treat problems such as anxiety and depression. It was through adapting this approach for

Activating event
Something happens
↓
Belief
Thoughts – what we believe about the event
↓
Consequence
Feelings and actions – how we feel about it and what we do next

FIGURE 1.3 **Albert Ellis' ABC model**

use on workplace training programs that the University of London researchers mentioned in the Introduction achieved such success with their resilience development programs. Today almost all resilience development interventions rely heavily on these techniques, which are covered in detail in later chapters.

Optimism

The characteristic of optimism is an aspect of positive belief that was identified many years ago as central to resilience. In his book on *Learned Optimism*,[39] first published in 1991, Martin Seligman expanded on the relationship between thoughts and feelings by differentiating between optimistic and pessimistic thinking styles. His early studies linked a pessimistic thinking style to "learned helplessness"—coming to believe through hardship that one is powerless to influence the events that determine well-being and success in life. The recognition that hardship often produces an opposite result—increased resilience—led to further studies and a more detailed understanding of what makes the difference between a positive and negative outcome. This work identified a factor known as explanatory or attributional style, which is the way everyone typically *explains* (in their own minds) what has happened, and specifically the extent to which they *attribute* positive or negative events to personal qualities that are long-lasting and that apply to many different situations.

To illustrate, a person who is naturally inclined to think "that was lucky" whenever something goes well, is probably not giving themselves due credit for the role played by their personal skills or abilities (at least on some of these occasions). It is easy to see how this could undermine their resilience, since it would imply seeing themselves as being dependent on luck rather than on the strengths they bring to the situation. Thinking "that was lucky" is not a problem if it happens only occasionally. However, someone who thinks something similar, every time they experience a successful outcome, definitely has an unhelpful negative bias in their explanatory style.

When it comes to unsuccessful or disappointing outcomes, on the other hand, a tendency to think "that was *unlucky*" is helpful for one's resilience, as long as the person concerned is realistic about any mistakes they have made and open to learning from them (with all of this, the key is *realistic*, positive thinking!). Thoughts such as "that was unlucky" reflect recognition of the temporary, situational factors at play and protect people from being too hard on themselves. In the context of bad events, the protective factor is less to do with locus of control (within or outside one's own control), and more to do with being able to see the cause of the problem as limited to that particular time and situation. The most damaging thoughts are deeply held negative beliefs about oneself that one is often hardly aware of, such as, "I just can't get to grips with things as quickly as other people" or "I'm always so disorganised." People who think like this believe that they will drag the causes of their problems with them wherever they go and whatever they do in the future. No wonder such thoughts undermine their resilience!

So, the key to understanding the difference between optimistic and pessimistic styles is analyzing how each person typically thinks about their successes and about their disappointments or failures. The great news is that workplace resilience training programs, such as the University of London courses mentioned earlier, have proven to be effective in helping participants to improve their explanatory style—with direct benefits for well-being, performance, and other positive outcomes. Chapter 4 provides detail on the kind of techniques used in these programs.

Permanent (always the case, now and in the future)	Temporary (likely to change in future)
Internal (due to me)	External (due to someone or something else)
Global (affects everything)	Specific (affects only this situation)

FIGURE 1.4   **The three dimensions of explanatory style**

SUCCESSES	
Positive explanatory style	**Negative explanatory style**
Permanent (always the case, now and in the future)	Temporary (likely to change in future)
Internal (due to me)	External (due to someone or something else)
Global (affects everything)	Specific (affects only this situation)

FIGURE 1.5   **The most positive and most negative explanatory styles for success**

FAILURES OR DISAPPOINTMENTS	
Positive explanatory style	**Negative explanatory style**
Temporary (likely to change in future)	Permanent (always the case, now and in the future)
External or Internal	Internal (due to me)
Specific (affects only this situation)	Global (affects everything)

FIGURE 1.6 **The most positive and most negative explanatory styles for failure**

Example—a successful outcome: my presentation was well received

Thought/belief about why this happened				Positivity rating
I prepared well for once	T	I	S	Low
I like to make sure I'm well prepared for presentations	P	I	S	Moderate
I'm good at preparing for things	P	I	G	High

Example—a disappointing outcome: our bid was unsuccessful

Thought/belief about why this happened				Positivity rating
I didn't spend as much time as usual on checking the detail	T	I	S	High
My colleague didn't spend enough time checking the detail	T	E	S	High
I'm not good under time pressure	P	I	G	Low
I find tender documents difficult to understand	P	I	S	Moderate

In Paul Costa and Robert McCrae's version of the FFM (the NEO PI-R, and the latest version, the NEO PI-3), optimism is most strongly represented in the *Extraversion* trait of *Positive Emotions* (optimism, enthusiasm), while pessimism is associated with the *Neuroticism* scale (anxiety, depression etc.) and negative affect (negative emotion). This reflects the research finding that although optimism and pessimism are clearly related, the underlying personality characteristics associated with optimistic and pessimistic thinking are not direct, polar opposites.[40] Introverts who are emotionally stable (low on *Neuroticism*) may be rather serious and "downbeat" in style, without believing that things will generally turn out badly. Conversely, a "neurotic extravert" may be full of anxiety and become discouraged quite easily, but then bounce back again quickly in response to a positive turn of events or even just a new perspective on the problem.

Self-belief and confidence

The work on explanatory style demonstrates clearly how important self-confidence is for resilience. It also shows how this needs to be true confidence in oneself and one's abilities, and not just a sense of confidence that one displays to the outside world. *Explanatory style* relates to a person's most firmly held beliefs about their ability to influence events—for better or worse. When the term "self-belief" is used in the context of resilience, it generally implies a deep-rooted, enduring belief in one's ability to tackle tough challenges, hold one's own among peers, and achieve success in whatever is taken on—influencing events for the better.

Looking at Table 1.1, we can see a number of related concepts listed: positive self-concept, self-enhancing biases, self-esteem, self-confidence/self-efficacy. These concepts are clearly similar, but the differences are not just semantic. When we look at the "OCEAN" FFM framework (Figure 1.2), we can see how the behavior we describe as confidence is actually influenced by a number of traits from different personality clusters—as illustrated in Table 1.2.

Some of these FFM traits are directly related to resilience through self-belief. *Competence*, for example, has been shown to be closely associated with self-esteem and internal locus of control.[41] Other traits in Table 1.2 are associated with confidence and resilience, but in a less direct way. In the case of *Assertiveness*, less extraverted people often hold back in a conversation simply because they are not driven to push themselves forward and are inclined to wait until they have something important to say. While there may, of course, be times when keeping quiet is the most adaptive response to the situation, in general assertive people are likely to have more control over events, and such control is a contributing factor to resilient outcomes. Once

Table 1.2　Some FFM traits associated with self-confidence

NEO PI-R facet scale (specific trait)	Appears to lack confidence	Appears confident	FFM Personality Factor (NEO PI-R broad trait)
Self-Consciousness (n4)	Shy, self-conscious, easily embarrassed	Socially confident, self-assured in interacting with others	Neuroticism (N)
Vulnerability to Stress (n6)	Feeling unable to cope; dependent or hopeless in stressful situations	Seeing oneself as capable of tackling difficult or potentially stressful situations	Neuroticism (N)
Assertiveness (e3)	Prefer to sit back and let others take the lead	Forceful, dominant; willing to speak out and take the lead	Extraversion (E)
Positive Emotions (e6)	Serious, inclined to downplay the possibilities in a situation	Cheerful, enthusiastic, optimistic about possibilities	Extraversion (E)
Compliance (a4)	Afraid of conflict, reluctant to stand firm	Competitive, demanding, can be stubborn	Agreeableness (A)
Modesty (a5)	Modest, humble, self-effacing	Seeing oneself as superior to others; arrogant	Agreeableness (A)
Competence (c1)	Uncertain about one's abilities; often feel ineffective	A strong sense of one's own capability and effectiveness	Conscientiousness (C)

again we see how the relationship between personality and resilience is neither simple nor linear.

Meaning and sense of purpose

While most people would intuitively associate self-confidence with resilience, the importance of having a strong sense of meaning or purpose has often been overlooked. "Meaning" in this context generally refers to a strongly held belief system about faith, the future, and the meaning of life. There are many accounts in literature of situations in which such beliefs were critical to resilience and survival—for example in Victor Frankl's book, *Man's Search for Meaning*,[42] about living in a Nazi concentration camp. Of course, this is a two-edged sword, as when such belief systems are challenged and broken by traumatic experiences this can have a negative effect on resilience that is difficult to repair.

"Sense of purpose" is a term often used for a more everyday version of meaning. It can refer to a wide range of goals, from long-term career aspirations to short-term objectives that provide people with a useful sense of structure and direction. All can help to boost someone's resilience, as long as they identify with the goals and view them as both reasonable and attainable.

Personal characteristics—a new perspective

In reviewing common themes that have emerged around the personal characteristics associated with resilience, we have begun to develop the case for a new perspective by drawing out the following points:

- There is a complex and non-linear relationship between personality traits on the one hand, and resilience processes and outcomes on the other. For example, being friendly and compliant can have a protective function in some situations, but in other situations standing firm is a more resilient thing to do.
- This implies that few personality traits are always good or always bad for resilience. Even anxiety, which is generally associated with susceptibility to stress, has an important role to play in ensuring one remains alert to danger and takes pre-emptive action. It would

be wrong to assume that the least anxious person is always the most resilient, irrespective of the situation.

- Clearly, it is important to consider the context when seeking to understand whether certain personal characteristics are likely to support or undermine someone's resilience. In particular, it is important to think about how individuals are likely to respond to different workplace pressures, depending on their personality, beliefs, attitudes, and abilities.
- Some of the concepts proposed as personality characteristics by resilience researchers are more like processes or outcomes, and are predicted by a number of different traits, attitudes, and abilities. An example is "ego resiliency," which is defined as the capacity to cope with adversity, and which has been found to be associated with behavior that is warm, friendly, empathic, and confident.
- The Five-Factor Model (FFM, NEO PI-R version) is a robust, well-researched framework that provides a comprehensive description of personality in terms of 36 specific traits clustered into five broad factors. This is a useful framework for exploring how specific traits relate to resilience through complex skills or processes like "emotional intelligence" and "self-regulation." It provides a useful guide to which elements of the mix are enduring traits and abilities, and which are skills and strategies that can be developed.

Hopefully in the future, more studies will be carried out specifically to investigate the relationship between the FFM and resilience. So far there have been relatively few, but the findings have generally demonstrated clear relationships in line with what might be expected on the basis of previous research and the authors' hypotheses. For example, Barbara Fredrickson and her colleagues[43] found a significant correlation between resilience and *Neuroticism* (a negative relationship with high resilience being associated with low *Neuroticism*). They also found statistically significant relationships between resilience and *Extraversion* (high resilience, high *Extraversion*) and between resilience and *Openness to Experience* (high resilience, high *Openness to Experience*). Other studies found a significant relationship between both *Extraversion* and *Emotional Stability* (low *Neuroticism*) on the one hand, and resilience on the other.[44]

Combining our understanding of the structure of individual differences and our knowledge of resilience-building processes, we have grouped the personal skills and attributes commonly identified by

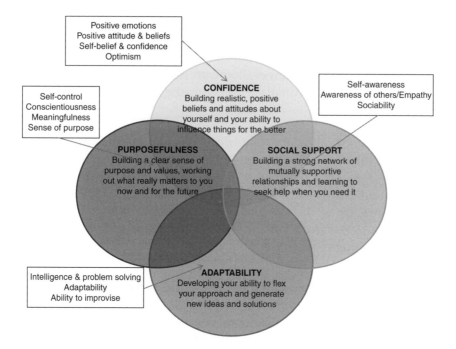

FIGURE 1.7 **Building resilience: the four personal resilience resources (showing relationship with the common personal attribute themes from resilience research)**

resilience researchers into four broad, overlapping clusters (Figure 1.7). Each cluster represents a *personal resilience resource* that can be developed using the approaches described in later chapters. This is a framework that we have been using for several years, for example, in the *i-resilience* questionnaire[45] and its associated resilience-building interventions.

MEASURING PERSONAL RESILIENCE

Where does this leave things in relation to assessing and developing employee resilience? Taking assessment to begin with, if you are to predict how your new colleague Petra will cope with pressure at work, you need to know about:

- what she brings with her to the situation, in the form of:
  - her personal resilience resources, represented by

41

- enduring traits and abilities;
- the skills and coping strategies she has developed over the years.
  - her wider circumstances (home pressures, family support etc.).
- The nature of the workplace pressures she faces and what support is available to her.

What you know about her out-of-work situation will always quite rightly be limited, and will in any case be subject to constant change. The question about personal resilience resources (enduring characteristics and skills) is, however, a useful one to ask. In addition, from your knowledge of the role and organizational context, you can try to work out what pressures she will typically face and what kind of support she might expect.

Resilience, competency-based performance, and assessment

Put like this, predicting how someone is likely to cope with pressure in a particular role or work context is no different from predicting other performance-related outcomes. Indeed, although talk of "resilience" is relatively new in most organizations, a cursory analysis of almost any good competency framework will reveal its presence. This may be either in the form of a whole competency (e.g. Personal Strength or Managing Pressure), or at the behavioral indicator level (e.g. "maintains quality of work under pressure" or "exercises good self-control in the face of frustration"). These competencies and indicators are equivalent to the personal resilience resources that people bring to the job, and we can use the same range of methods to assess them—including competency-based interviews, psychometric assessment, and a range of exercises.

For purposes of recruitment and selection, we generally recommend incorporating resilience into your competency-based assessment procedures. In this way, you could be sure that resilience as you are measuring it is relevant to the role in question—one of the essential requirements for a fair and robust selection process. This approach would involve using one of the recognized job or competency analysis techniques to define specific requirements and behavioral criteria related to coping in a resilient way with typical challenges of the role. The next step would be to adapt your interview and other assessment procedures to measure the new criteria.

Personality profiling can play a useful role in this context, although it should, of course, never be used on its own to make final judgments. Situational Judgment Tests also have the potential to provide useful insights into resilience-related requirements.[46]

Research-based measures of adult resilience

There are a number of specific resilience assessment tools that have been developed based on up-to-date resilience research, and established as valid measures of resilience in a wide range of contexts. Many of them are self-report measures with items that are very open and transparent, making it likely that they would be subject to motivational distortion/impression management in a selection situation.

Taking such considerations into account, it seems likely that these measures would be more useful and appropriate in the context of resilience-building interventions. So, what instruments are currently available and suitable for use in the workplace? A review of resilience measurement scales published in 2011 found "no current 'gold standard' amongst 15 measures of resilience"[47] and highlighted the need for a greater selection of well-designed and validated measures to suit different groups and contexts. The authors of the review make the point that the complex problem of how to define resilience—as discussed in this chapter—has created quite a challenge for anyone interested in measuring it.

Many of the available measures are designed specifically for children, adolescents, or young adults. Table 1.3 provides a brief overview of some of the best-performing adult measures included in the 2011 review. All those listed are self-report questionnaire measures.

Other questionnaires have been developed to measure specific theoretical constructs such as Ego Resiliency[48] and Attributional Style (Seligman's Attributional Style Questionnaire—SASQ).[49]

Resilience measures for the work context

With the recent growth of interest in resilience at work, a number of resilience measures have been developed with this context in mind (see Table 1.4).

Table 1.3 **Some of the best-performing measures of resilience in adults, as evaluated by Gill Windle and her colleagues in 2011**

Measure	Authors	Approach
The Resilience Scale for Adults (RSA—various versions)	Friborg and others, 2003, 2005	Based on research into key features of resilient people (personal characteristics, family etc.)
The Connor–Davidson Resilience Scale (CD-RISC)	Connor and Davidson, 2003	Developed to assess ability to cope with stress; based on resilience as a personal quality (made up of five factors)
The Brief Resilience Scale	Smith and others, 2008	Outcome-focused, measuring recovery ability rather than protective factors
Psychological Resilience	Windle and others, 2008	Developed as a model of psychological resilience, assessing the protective factors of self-esteem, personal competence, and interpersonal control
The Resilience Scale (RS)	Wagnild and Young, 1993	Personality-based, measuring individual resilience in terms of personal competence, and acceptance of self and life

The use of diagnostic instruments such as these to assess one's personal resilience is picked up again in Chapter 4, where we discuss what individuals can do to improve their resilience. Assessing what we call "your personal resilience starting point" is the first step in the development process. Completing one or two of the questionnaires or other measures listed above can be very useful in helping to take stock of the individual side of the equation—the natural resilience strengths and risks that each of us brings with us. There is, however, another side to this equation—that of the situation. As resilience-building is a process and not just a set of personal traits, we need to understand the role of the circumstances we find ourselves in, both at work and outside it.

As we saw in Figure 1.1, it is the interaction between a person's situation on the one hand, and their underlying personality and abilities on the other, that gives rise to the process of building (or

Table 1.4 **Some measures of resilience developed specifically with workplace challenges in mind**

Measure	Author(s)	Approach
Ashridge Resilience Questionnaire (ARQ) ashridge.org.uk	Alex Davda, Ashridge	Designed to help managers take stock of their personal resilience through understanding their perceived ability to respond to a stressful situation. Resilience is measured by six core attitudes; Emotional Control, Self-Belief, Purpose, Adapting to Change, Awareness of Others and Balancing Alternatives. The ARQ is not a formal assessment; it is intended to form the basis for thought, reflection, and conversation.
The Dispositional Resilience Scale hardinessinstitute.com	Paul Bartone, Hardiness Institute	Designed to measure psychological hardiness (the 3Cs of commitment, control, and challenge).
i-resilience robertsoncooper.com	Jill Flint-Taylor, Alex Jansen-Birch, and Ivan Robertson, Robertson Cooper Ltd	Self-report measure of the Five-Factor Model of personality—output in the form of a research-based expert system development report suggesting likely personal strengths and risks in relation to the four components of resilience (Confidence, Social Support, Adaptability and Purposefulness) and the six ASSET factors (sources of workplace pressure and support).
Mental Toughness Questionnaire (MTQ48) aqr.co.uk	Peter Clough and colleagues AQR Ltd	Assesses ability to withstand pressure in a range of environments, measuring mental toughness in terms of four core components—control, challenge, commitment, and confidence.

Continued

Table 1.4 Continued

Measure	Author(s)	Approach
Resilience Assessment Questionnaire (RAQ) mas.org.uk	Derek Mowbray, MAS (Management Advisory Service), and Organisation Health Psychologists	A staff resilience survey designed to assess how resilient the workforce is against threats to well-being and performance.
Resilience at Work (RAW) scale workingwithresilience. com.au	Peter Winwood and Kathryn McEwen	Based on the principle that resilience can be taught. Measures seven factors identified through the theory of work-related strain effects and practitioner experience in work capacity optimization and work stress minimization.
The Resilience Factor Inventory http://adaptivlearning.com	Andrew Shatte and Karen Reivich; Adaptiv Learning Systems and The Hay Group	A diagnostic tool to measure individual resilience—the Resilience Factor Inventory (RFI) and an associated workbook. A 60-item, multi-rater 360° feedback instrument, which provides self, manager, direct report, and peer feedback on seven critical factors—or inner strengths: Emotion Regulation, Impulse Control, Causal Analysis, Self-Efficacy, Realistic Optimism, Empathy, Reaching Out.
The Resilience Questionnaire adc.uk.com	A&DC	Structured in terms of eight elements that assess thought patterns, preferences, and behavior that affect an individual's ability to respond positively to challenges and setbacks.

undermining) their personal resilience resources. So the following chapter is devoted to the question of the situation (in particular the work situation) and to practical illustrations of the interaction between individual and situation. Part 2 provides a detailed discussion of how resilience can be improved.

CHAPTER 2

"THE INDIVIDUAL + THE SITUATION"—PERSONAL RESILIENCE AT WORK

UNDERSTANDING PRESSURE IN THE WORKPLACE

In Chapter 1, we explored the individual side of the equation presented in Figure 2.1, and we summarized these resources by grouping them into four broad clusters: *Confidence, Social Support, Adaptability*

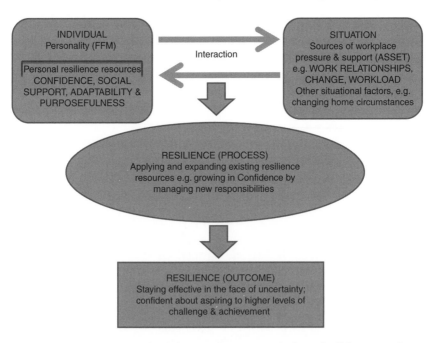

FIGURE 2.1 **How on-the-job experiences can help to build personal resilience**

and *Purposefulness*. This sets the foundation for individuals to evaluate the existing state of their personal resilience resources. We also provided an overview of some of the available measures of adult resilience, most of which tap into all four components to some extent. This brings us to a more detailed exploration of the other side of the picture—the situation, and in particular the work context.

THE WORKPLACE SITUATION—SOURCES OF PRESSURE AND SUPPORT

Chapter 3 provides an in-depth account of how resilience development fits within the history of stress management in organizations, demonstrating how the emphasis has shifted in recent years towards a more strategic well-being agenda. This is the context in which the research-based ASSET framework[1] has been developed and updated over the years. Here we use the ASSET framework (Figure 2.2) to facilitate our analysis of the interplay between different personal resilience resources and the range of challenges people face at work. Having used it for several years in our own coaching and development practice, we have found that the framework enables people to chunk the pressure they face at work. As always, breaking a problem

Main sources of pressure and support in the workplace (ASSET factors): defined in terms of optimum conditions
Resources and communication   Visible leadership, good provision of information, resources and development
Control   Having a voice and influence over what is done and how
Work life balance + Workload   Healthy balance between work and home life; challenging but manageable work demands
Job security and change   Organizational change is stimulating, helpful and well-managed
Work relationships   Relationships constructive and collaborative but also stimulating/challenging
Job conditions   An interesting, stimulating role with motivational rewards and working conditions

FIGURE 2.2 **Summary of the ASSET framework for measuring sources of pressure and support in the workplace**

down into chunks makes it easier to manage—in this case by considering which pressures pose the greatest challenge or risk for each of us, and how best to mobilize our personal resilience resources to ensure a good outcome. This process is facilitated by recognizing that sources of pressure, such as work relationships, can also be sources of support for us to draw on.

Sources of negative pressure (stress)

To begin with, we look at how the six ASSET factors operate as sources of negative pressure with the potential to cause stress, especially in the absence of good resilience management skills. As mentioned previously, pressure turns to stress at the point we believe we are no longer able to cope with it. Below are some examples of specific issues and how they relate to the six main factors.

The specific issues set out in Figure 2.3 are all known to be common sources of stress and have, therefore, formed part of our organizational well-being audits for many years. Some hardly need explaining—we can probably all relate to the idea that working with faulty or out-of-date equipment can be very stressful. Others may not be something you would immediately think of in relation to stress, but it is surprising how often they turn up as a problem pressure point in an otherwise well-managed team. "Being upset by others taking the credit for what you have achieved" is one of these. It is not something people would generally think to include when putting together a set of "stress lens" questions for an annual staff survey, but it is common, very damaging to employee morale and well-being when it happens on a regular basis, and often quite hard for managers to spot and address. Dull and repetitive work is another one. It may not look stressful to the casual observer, but reflecting on it for a moment, we can see how easily it could become so for someone who feels trapped with no opportunity to develop their skills or to achieve something worthwhile.

Lack of control—the stress "super-factor"

Then there is the issue of control—or the lack of it—which deserves a special mention as it is almost a stress "super-factor." Feeling that we

Aggressive management style and the issue of bullying

Nowhere is the interaction between the individual and their work situation more complicated and fraught than in the area of aggressive management style and bullying. Most people would probably agree with the definition of bullying as an act of repeated aggressive behavior undertaken in order to *intentionally hurt* another person, physically or mentally—when someone behaves in a certain way to gain power over another person.[2] Seen in this light, someone behaving in a forceful or demanding manner is not necessarily a bully, even if their behavior results in another person feeling stressed.

However, we frequently come across situations where managers are labeled bullies when the reality is that they simply do not have the skills to manage performance effectively, and their conscientious attempts to do so result in stress for others—and often for the managers too. This is a common but truly tragic situation for all involved—managers must take responsibility for the impact of their actions, but are they bullies if they have no intention to cause harm?

Even in the course of everyday discussions about how the work should be done, some people may experience a manager's energy and enthusiasm as pushy and intimidating, while others find it encouraging and motivating. In other situations, the issue may be stress due to a perceived lack of control—which can result from a wide range of factors both within and outside the manager's sphere of influence. In terms of resilience and the interaction between the person (team member) and situation (manager's behavior), people with a negative thinking style are more likely to jump to negative conclusions about what is in their manager's head. It's always hard to get at people's true attitudes, beliefs, and intentions. However, if a charge of bullying is on the cards then it is absolutely essential to try to understand what has been going through the minds of both parties.

have little power to influence decisions or events—especially those which could potentially have a direct and negative impact on us—is one of the main causes of pressure turning to stress. As long as we believe there is some action we can take to improve our situation, it is easier to keep stress at bay. For this reason, one of the most powerful stress management strategies is learning to take control through the way you view and respond to the situation (the Cognitive–Behavioral approach, explained in more detail in Chapter 4). Some people unintentionally cause a problem for themselves in this area, by consistently under-estimating their ability to steer or influence what happens. They may be described as having an *external locus of control*, or a negative explanatory style—as explained in the previous chapter. For others, the trouble starts when they perceive that something about a particular situation is preventing them from making a contribution to plans and decisions, or from having their say in how their work is done.

A common example would be a situation where the manager of a team is so sure of being right, that he or she fails to involve team members in making plans, or ends up discounting their suggestions when making the final decision. Managers who have a very strong belief in their own capability and judgment often do this without appreciating the stress it can cause for team members. A member of the team who is at the other end of the spectrum—who lacks confidence in their ability to influence events—is at an immediate disadvantage in this situation as they may feel it is not even worthwhile trying. A colleague with stronger self-belief, on the other hand, may feel frustrated but still prepared to question the manager's decisions or actions. If they do, they have created another opportunity to influence the decision and they may well be successful, as over-confident managers often do not mean to create stress in the team—they simply push on without realizing the risks, because they believe they know best.

This illustration shows that, when faced with a situation where their ability to influence events is compromised, a person's response and the outcome both depend on their "personal resilience resources." More specifically, it shows the importance of "self-belief" for ensuring they retain a level of control over events that affect them—and that both too much and too little self-belief can cause problems. Nevertheless, self-belief is only one factor underpinning resilience. In another situation, the person who lacks self-belief may prove surprisingly resilient in dealing with pressure of a different kind. If, for example, he or she has a sociable, empathic style and a strong network of supportive relationships, they may draw on this to avoid becoming stressed in a job that involves dealing with difficult customers on a regular basis. These points are explored in more depth in the individual case studies later.

Why do we refer to control as a stress "super-factor"? We do so partly because it is linked to one of the most effective stress management

Main sources of pressure and support in the workplace	Negative pressures pushing us over the top into burn-out
Resources and communication	e.g. infrequent feedback and communication, inadequate training; out-of-date technology, equipment or resources
Control	e.g. ideas not listened to; lack of control over job and decisions, performance targets imposed rather than collaboratively created
Work life balance: Workload	e.g. unreasonable expectations; round-the-clock emailing; too much time travelling, too little time to complete tasks, work unreasonably interfering with home life
Job security and change	e.g. job insecurity; fear of skill redundancy; change for change's sake
Work relationships	e.g. aggressive management style; others taking credit for your achievements, isolation and/or lack of support from others
Job conditions	e.g. inequalities or lack of transparency in remuneration and benefits; dull and repetitive work; difficult customers

FIGURE 2.3   **The ASSET factors—examples of negative pressure**

strategies, as mentioned above. In addition, an examination of the other examples in Figure 2.3 will show that one of the reasons many of them are potentially stressful is because they take away people's ability to influence events and actively manage the situation to avoid a negative outcome for themselves, their colleagues, and even their families. Take the example of "infrequent feedback and communication"—in practice concerns about this typically stem from anxiety that your boss or other senior managers are not keeping you in the picture about your own performance and/or plans that are likely to affect your future. As everyone knows, "information is power," and without it you are disadvantaged in your attempts to meet objectives, further your career, establish a secure future for yourself and your family, and so on. The issue is similar when people are troubled by a lack of transparency in remuneration and benefits—given transparency, people feel better equipped to judge whether the situation is unfair, and to take action by arguing their case or looking for another job.

Resilient people are those who manage pressure effectively, but it is difficult to do this if you do not have enough of the facts. The most resilient will tolerate this for only so long before taking control back by moving out of the situation altogether. This is why organizations lose many of their best people during times of uncertainty and change. In such situations resilient people rarely leave because they are too anxious about the uncertainty, or too lacking in self-confidence to believe there will be a job for them. They go because they prefer to be in control, and because their confident, proactive approach makes it easier for them to find alternative employment.

It should be clear from the above discussion that "control" in this context is not about needing to exercise "command and control" over other people, or being the one who has the final say in all decisions. For most people it is sufficient to have a clear picture of what is happening or being planned, and enough room to apply both that information and their own ideas to good effect.

The "provision of information" is a good example of how managers can often achieve a "quick win" in supporting employees' resilience. Sometimes information is withheld deliberately, but more often managers just forget that team members are not in the same meetings as they are and simply do not have access to the same information. Recognizing how this can lead to stress and making an effort to provide as much clear, concise, and relevant information as possible, is one of the best things a manager can do to help individuals make the most of their personal resilience resources.

Sources of positive pressure (challenge pressure)

Many sources of pressure can be either positive or negative, depending on the circumstances and the person experiencing the pressure. Work targets are one of the most obvious examples of this. Team members may feel differently about being given the same sales target, for example. Frank may feel that the target is challenging and motivating, while Charlie feels stressed and demotivated. There are many reasons for such differences, including each person's personal circumstances, the training they have had, what they think about the current economic climate, what they think about their own abilities, their experience of past success, their relationship with their manager and colleagues, the number of active leads they have, and so on. One way or another, Frank probably believes the target is realistic and achievable—even if he recognizes this may be difficult and success is not to be taken for granted. Charlie probably believes that the target is out of reach, or that too much will have to be sacrificed in order to achieve it.

It can also happen that the source of pressure is viewed differently by the same person at different times. Frank may have embraced the target with energy and enthusiasm to start with, then lost momentum and become dispirited in a way that his manager finds hard to account for. What she is unaware of is that Frank's marriage is in trouble. This is causing him stress and sleepless nights, and he no longer feels he has the energy to put in the effort needed to achieve the target—he no longer sees it as achievable, even though the target and his work situation have not changed. This is one of the things that makes it so difficult for managers to "keep pressure positive" for those who report to them—not only does each member of the team respond differently to the same sources of pressure, but each person also responds differently depending on what is going on both at work and outside it.

We have described how a lack of control over events can be a major source of negative pressure and stress. So is there a sense in which having control can be a positive pressure? There is, and it generally takes the form of responsibility. Most people welcome some level of responsibility at work for the positive challenge pressure it brings, although the level of responsibility each feels comfortable with varies hugely. People who seek and succeed in senior management positions typically thrive on a high level of responsibility. They like to feel stretched and they feel sufficiently confident in their ability to cope with the pressure it brings—although as we have seen, confidence is very complex and the best leaders experience doubts at times. The positive aspects of control and responsibility help to explain a very common finding in our stress auditing work, that is, clients are often surprised to find junior staff reporting higher levels of stress than the senior group. When we look at the detail in such cases, one of the most common explanations is that the senior group has the positive

Main sources of pressure and support in the workplace	Positive pressures bringing us up the pressure/performance curve
Resources and communication	e.g. a leader with an inspiring vision; exciting career development opportunities
Control	e.g. responsibility for making key decisions; involvement in making improvements
Work life balance: Workload	e.g. challenging but realistic deadlines; difficult but important problems to solve; desire to balance work and home life
Job security and change	e.g. new systems and processes that bring clear benefits; new job opportunities
Work relationships	e.g. constructive debate and/or healthy competition within the team
Job conditions	e.g. motivational bonus scheme; stimulating and varied work; demanding but appreciative manager and customers

FIGURE 2.4 **The ASSET factors—examples of positive pressure**

challenge of responsibility combined with sufficient influence over plans and events to feel in control. We often find that the junior staff groups who are reporting stress feel that they may have less responsibility but they also have far less influence or control over how they fulfill those responsibilities. They may even be bored, frustrated, and stressed at the same time!

What about "workload" and "work life balance"—how can these be positive sources of pressure? In the context of pressure, workload is typically seen as a bad thing. However, many people know what it feels like to be under-occupied at work. This is not just a matter of responsibility—some people like to be very busy at work even though they are happy doing routine tasks and do not seek a high level of responsibility. Some people need the workload to build up before they feel energized to tackle it—they become demotivated if the work demands are low and the pace is slow, and enjoy the challenge pressure of having a lot to achieve within a short time-frame. The desire for a good work life balance can also be a positive pressure—although it can be tough to fit the work into a manageable number of hours, many people are motivated by the challenge and the reward of having to make time to spend with family and friends. As always, the tipping point from positive into negative pressure is when you see the challenge as too difficult, unreasonable, or unrealistic.

In these times of constant organizational change, it can sometimes be hard to picture change as a positive pressure. Yet many people thrive on it—as Robert Safian described in his Fast Company feature titled "This Is Generation Flux: Meet The Pioneers Of The New (and Chaotic) Frontier Of Business."[3] In this article Safian gives detailed illustrations of important social, economic, and technological contributions being made by people who thrive on complexity and rapid change.

Work relationships are clearly an important source of support, yet they too can be seen as a source of positive, challenge pressure. A typical scenario here would be wanting to do your best for a team that you enjoy being part of, or for a boss you feel has treated you very well over the years. In the case of demanding clients, many of the best relationship managers are motivated by the effort and skill required to meet or exceed the clients' complex needs and high expectations.

Sources of support

A "source of challenge pressure" is obviously very different from a "source of support," even though the two are typically associated with positive rather than negative outcomes. We say typically, since just as challenge pressure can turn into hindrance pressure in a moment as circumstances and perceptions shift, so too sources of support can become a liability at times. This may be because someone puts themselves at risk by over-relying on certain sources of support. It could also be a result of unintended consequences that sometimes arise when support is provided—for example when a manager encourages a supportive, consensus-driven team climate at the expense of allowing constructive challenge, and the kind of debate that fuels innovation and

Main sources of pressure and support in the workplace	*Support* helping to keep us at the top of the curve
Resources and communication	e.g. good communication practices; well-resourced IT support
Control	e.g. manager uses team meetings to gather input – and takes this into account
Work life balance: **Workload**	e.g. flexible working policies and practices; clarity of manager's expectations and guidance on priorities
Job security and change	e.g. training in new skills ; consultation on implementation of change
Work relationships	e.g. colleagues sharing the workload when someone is absent; sharing expertise
Job conditions	e.g. transparency in remuneration and benefits; a clean, bright work environment; recognition of success

FIGURE 2.5   **The ASSET factors—examples of support**

achievement. In such a team people may feel safe and comfortable to start with, but then become frustrated at the lack of challenge, debate, and opportunity to prove themselves. For the more competitive and ambitious among us, this could quickly turn to anger and stress.

So there is such a thing as too much support, or the wrong kind of support. In general, however, support is a positive element in the work environment, and one that resilient people play an active part in building for themselves and often for others too. The six ASSET factors can also be used to categorize the main sources of support, as shown in Figure 2.5. In stress and resilience terms, the most important sources of support tend to be those that are identified in their absence by higher levels of stress—such as good communication, high quality training provision, and constructive feedback.

THE FFM AND THE SOURCES OF
WORKPLACE PRESSURE AND SUPPORT

So what is it about an individual that drives these differences in whether he or she experiences pressure as positive or negative, and whether they build and make use of a strong social support network? Is it a question of their circumstances plus a few of the right "resilience qualities," like self-belief? Or do they need to consider how their personality affects their resilience in a more holistic way, by looking at the implications of all their personality traits for the way they interact with their situation at work and outside it? We believe the latter. Although we recognize that certain characteristics such as *Confidence* and *Emotional Stability* are more important for resilience than others, we consider it useful to reflect on the implications of all traits even where the connection is less obvious. For example, *Sense of Duty* can clearly be associated with *Purposefulness*, while *Openness to Emotional Experience* can be helpful in building relationships and strengthening *Social Support*.

In the previous chapter, we touched on the relationships between the FFM personality framework, competency-based assessment, and resilience outcomes. Here we show how the FFM framework of what each person brings to the work situation can be used to help in evaluating our own "resilience starting point"—setting the foundation for the very personal plan that each of us needs to begin raising our resilience to the next level.

The FFM does not measure resilience processes or outcomes

It is very important to emphasize that completing an FFM personality questionnaire will not provide a direct, comprehensive measure of someone's resilience. It does not tell us about the range of coping strategies that someone has learned to use over the years, nor does it provide evidence on how he or she actually behaves in the face of various work pressures. Its value lies instead in helping someone to take stock of the enduring character strengths that he or she brings with them into any situation, and how these strengths might relate to achieving resilient outcomes. It also helps them to identify and reflect on personal characteristics that could undermine their resilience at times, so they can watch out for this and make a conscious effort to manage these risks by challenging their own assumptions, adapting their behavior and taking pre-emptive action. As the FFM provides a comprehensive description of our enduring personality traits, and as personality can be seen as "master psychological system" (see Chapter 1), reviewing their own FFM profile helps a person to take a holistic view of the underlying strengths and risks they bring to the management of workplace pressures. It is only a starting point in a personal resilience development action plan, but it provides a very firm foundation. The next step is, of course, to consider what strategies and behaviors they have already put in place to make the most of these strengths and to help them manage the risks.

The question of strategies and behaviors is dealt with in detail in Part 2, which covers a wide range of practical resilience-building approaches. First, however, we illustrate how the FFM relates to the four resilience resources, and to the six sources of workplace pressure and support. We mentioned previously the research that we and others have done linking the FFM to competency-based performance. We also observed that resilience is often either implicitly or explicitly incorporated into organizations' competency frameworks, in the form of desired behaviors and performance-related outcomes.

Competency frameworks as a source of information on resilience at work

This is, in our view, a rich but generally under-used source of evidence on what underpins resilience at work, and how individuals are likely to respond to different work pressures. If the mere mention of the word "competency" makes you twitch, bear with us while we explain. Much could be said about the pros and cons of using a competency approach, and there is no doubt that whenever something becomes widely popular it also suffers from being over-engineered by the industry that profits from it. Nevertheless, the simple truth is that the past twenty years have seen a lasting shift to the use of specific, clearly defined behavioral criteria and evidence-based assessment, both for selection and development purposes—whether this is described in terms of competencies or not.

There are three ways in which the development and use of organizational competency frameworks (or other forms of behavioral criteria) can provide evidence-based insights into resilience at work:

- If a reputable competency analysis technique, such as the Behavioral Event Interview,[4] is used to define the framework in the first place, it can provide us with evidence of specific resilience requirements for different job demands and work contexts.
- The analysis of competency-based ratings from 360° feedback, assessment centers, and other sources provides greater understanding of the personal skills, attitudes, and other characteristics associated with successful work outcomes, including coping with pressure and adversity.
- Behavioral or competency-based assessments can be used to validate the use of the FFM and other psychometric measures for the prediction of work performance, helping to make the connection between personal characteristics on the one hand, and resilience processes and work-related outcomes on the other.

For various reasons, as we said, resilience researchers and practitioners have not made the most of the potential insights from these sources. There are exceptions, however. One of these is the work on emotional intelligence carried out by Daniel Goleman and his colleagues. Many people are aware that Goleman popularized the concept of emotional intelligence, and we have already shown how this concept has been taken up within the context of understanding resilience. Fewer people, however, are aware that Goleman's discussion of emotional intelligence at work was informed by the analysis of a vast bank of competency data collected by the Hay McBer consultancy group and their clients. In particular, this research sought to identify the characteristics that differentiated superior performers from their colleagues, and the results informed the way Goleman described emotional intelligence and related it to leadership and other work contexts.[5]

The original McBer organization was co-founded by psychologist David McClelland, who began to promote competency-based assessment in the early 1970s. McClelland was very critical of the over-reliance on intelligence testing that was prevalent at that time, especially in the United States.[6] The power and simplicity of his insights are often lost these days in the competency maze, especially as they now seem like common sense. However, at the time he had to fight hard to gain recognition of the idea that measuring intelligence (or reasoning ability) is useful but only gives you part of the picture. He was particularly interested in the way every person differs in his or her motivation or need for achievement. He argued that if you recruit someone purely on the basis of how well he or she does in an intelligence test, you know nothing about their motivation, i.e. how hard they are likely to try to achieve specific goals or success in general. Your new recruit may be smart enough to do the job, but will they make enough of an effort to do well?

To complete the picture, McClelland pointed out we should also measure "interpersonal skills," as these were clearly important for performance at work and did not seem to be related to intelligence or motivation. Subsequent research has shown that in nearly all well-defined competency frameworks there are three separate clusters of personal skills and qualities—to do with *reasoning/intellect, interpersonal skills* and *motivation* respectively. These clusters may or may not be immediately obvious through an examination of the different competency headings in a framework, but they emerge consistently from statistical analyses of the competency-based ratings that the organization collects over time.

Where resilience and related constructs are explicit in a competency framework, they often appear in the competencies that relate to the motivation cluster, e.g. "maintains a positive approach in the face of tough challenges." However, the discussion in Chapter 1 shows clearly how reasoning ability and interpersonal skills can be just as important for ensuring a resilient outcome. This is the background to why we have been able to incorporate our own and others' competency research into our understanding of resilience at work. These analyses form the basis for our hypotheses about how specific FFM traits might play out in relation to different sources of pressure in the work situation—as reflected in Robertson Cooper's *i-resilience* profiling measure and in the fictitious team scenario set out below.

THE GREEN ACCOUNTS TEAM: AN ILLUSTRATION OF INDIVIDUAL DIFFERENCES

In this section we put together a team's ASSET results and a number of individual FFM profiles to create a fictional team scenario. This illustrates how we can use the ASSET (workplace situation) and FFM

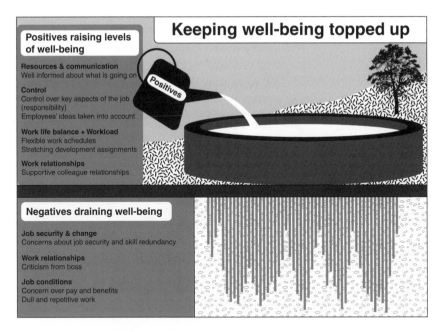

Keeping well-being topped up

Positives raising levels of well-being

Resources & communication
Well informed about what is going on

Control
Control over key aspects of the job (responsibility)
Employees' ideas taken into account

Work life balance + Workload
Flexible work schedules
Stretching development assignments

Work relationships
Supportive colleague relationships

Negatives draining well-being

Job security & change
Concerns about job security and skill redundancy

Work relationships
Criticism from boss

Job conditions
Concern over pay and benefits
Dull and repetitive work

FIGURE 2.6 **How the Green Accounts team see their situation—the factors topping up and draining their** *well-being reservoir* **(results of an ASSET audit)**

(individual personality) models to help understand how character differences interact with the work situation to influence people's responses to pressure.

The team

The Green Accounts team is part of a new department created following a merger between a large organization and a smaller one. The two merging organizations had very different cultures, and this is widely seen as a potential barrier to smooth integration. Across the Department there are noticeable tensions in work relationships, but the four members of the Green Accounts team generally get on well—Sarah, Xiu Bo, and Daniel are from the smaller organization and their colleague, Raj, joined the larger organization a year ago. The team is one of three reporting to Helena, a manager who has been with the larger organization for many years.

Sarah

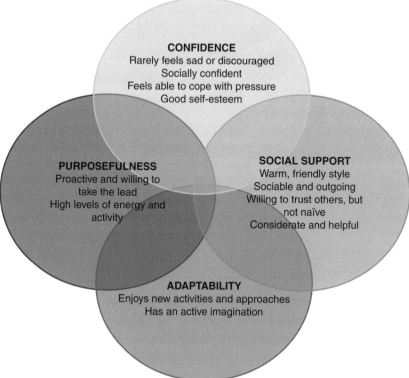

FIGURE 2.7 **How Sarah's character strengths relate to the four resilience resources (relationships overlap, e.g. Social Confidence relates mainly to Confidence but also to Social Support)**

Main risks in Sarah's natural style

Confidence: A dislike of conflict could undermine her confidence in taking a firm stand.

Adaptability: A high need for order and structure may make it difficult for her to respond flexibly to new developments.

Purposefulness: She sometimes finds it difficult to sustain her efforts and to finish what she starts.

Sarah and the current situation: Sarah has taken advantage of the opportunity to take on extra responsibility and stretching developmental assignments, and her confidence and morale have been boosted by the fact that she is doing well and learning new skills. Positive work relationships are very important to her and although she is anxious about the security of her job, she draws a lot of comfort from the supportive atmosphere amongst her team colleagues. On the other hand, she resents the critical style of her boss. She is annoyed with Helena and with herself for not standing up to her. Sarah is usually very quick to make her views known, but she prefers to avoid unpleasantness and hates the idea of getting into an argument with Helena.

Overall, the main impact of the current situation has been to improve Sarah's resilience by increasing her confidence and capability. As her self-esteem is good and as she has the support of her colleagues, her boss's critical style is causing her some stress but appears unlikely to have an enduring impact on her resilience unless the problem becomes more severe.

Xiu Bo

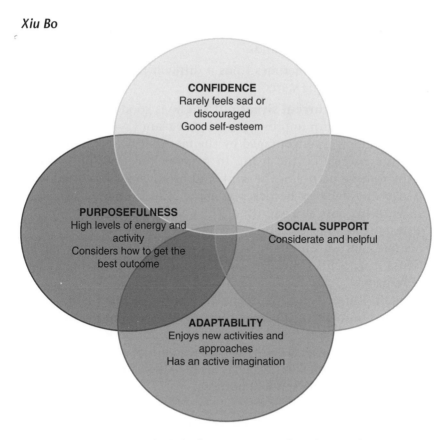

FIGURE 2.8   **How Xiu Bo's character strengths relate to the four resilience resources**

Main risks in Xiu Bo's natural style

Confidence: He is not particularly confident in his ability to manage potentially stressful situations.

Social Support: He is rather skeptical of others people's intentions, and careful about whom he trusts; this could limit his ability to draw on support when he needs it.

Adaptability: Being prone to feelings of irritability and impatience may make it difficult for him to deal with problems and everyday frustrations in a calm and flexible manner. He may put himself under pressure by giving in to his impulses rather than exercising self-control to respond in a constructive, adaptable way. He pays relatively little attention to emotional reactions, and may overlook some of the clues he needs to adapt to changing situations. Being very focused on specific, practical issues may limit his adaptability to different situations and demands.

Purposefulness: He sometimes finds it difficult to sustain his efforts and to finish what he starts.

Xiu Bo and the current situation: Xiu Bo is good at making practical suggestions for improvements to the team's systems and processes, and he feels encouraged by the fact that his ideas are often put into practice by the team. In general, however, he is bored by the routine nature of the work and he is very dissatisfied with his pay—he believes he deserves more. Unfortunately he raised this with his boss at a bad time. The ensuring argument left him frustrated and annoyed and since then he has let the matter drop. This left him unsure about what to do next—he is reluctant to discuss it with his colleagues, and has no idea whether they feel the same way.

Overall, Xiu Bo is feeling frustrated and stressed by his situation, but he has been giving it a lot of thought and is beginning to formulate a plan to change jobs. Unusually for him, he has spent time reflecting on how he feels. This has helped him to focus on what matters to him, which in the end is likely to increase his resilience by giving him a stronger sense of purpose.

Raj

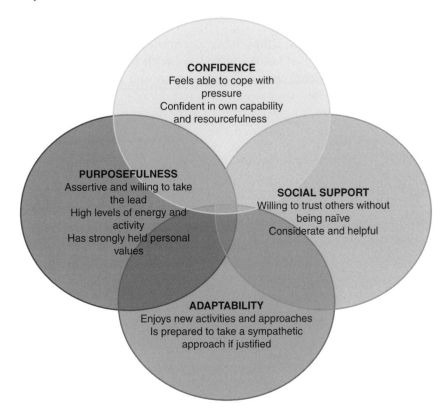

FIGURE 2.9   **How Raj's character strengths relate to the four resilience resources**

Main risks in Raj's natural style

Confidence: His attitude to life and work tends to be serious rather than light-hearted.

Social Support: He tends to be formal and reserved in his relationships, and may keep his distance from some of the people who could provide useful social support in difficult times.

Adaptability: Being prone to feelings of irritability and impatience may make it difficult for him to deal with problems and everyday frustrations in a calm and flexible manner.

Raj and the current situation: Like the rest of the team, Raj's attitude is considerate and helpful. This is a characteristic they all have

in common, so it is not surprising that "supportive colleague relationships" is one of the factors topping up the team's well-being
reservoir. Like Xiu Bo and Daniel, however, Raj can become quite
irritable or impatient at times. Also, his manner tends to be rather
cool and distant. This is not really an issue with his team colleagues,
who have learned that he cares about them and they can rely on
him for support when they need it. His impatience and reserve have,
however, had a rather negative impact recently on his ability to build
relationships with colleagues in the Customer Support team. In a
recent conversation with Helena, this was raised as a performance
issue—relationships with the Customer Support team being critical
but rather tricky for various reasons.

Overall, Raj has been angry for some time about what he sees as
Helena's negativity and lack of support, and he now feels that she is
unfairly putting obstacles in the way of his career progression. As he
shares the team's general concerns about rewards, insecurity, and the
unsatisfying nature of the work, he has decided the time has come to
have an open and honest conversation with Helena about his ambi-
tions and concerns. His resilience strengths are likely to stand him
in good stead in dealing with this situation, as long as he is able to
manage his frustration and take a calm, constructive approach to his
conversation with Helena.

Daniel

Main risks in Daniel's natural style

Confidence: When he is the focus of attention, feeling awkward
or self-conscious may undermine his confidence, especially when
dealing with people he does not know very well. He is not particularly confident in his ability to manage potentially stressful
situations. A dislike of conflict could undermine his confidence
in taking a firm stand. He tends to be modest and unassum-
ing; he may be uncomfortable talking about his successes and
achievements.

Adaptability: Being prone to feelings of irritability and impatience
may make it difficult for him to deal with problems and everyday
frustrations in a calm and flexible manner. Preferring to keep to
what he knows may affect the flexibility of his response to change
and new situations.

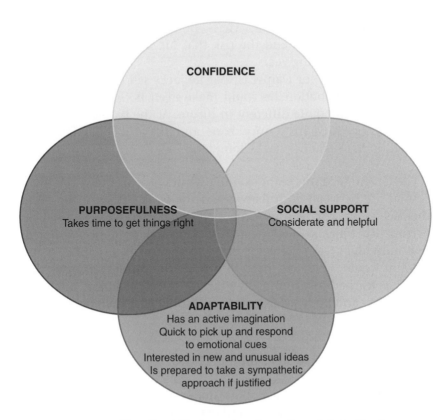

FIGURE 2.10 **How Daniel's character strengths relate to the four resilience resources**

Purposefulness: The pace he sets is likely to be measured rather than busy and energetic. He is likely to be quite casual about adhering to ethical principles and fulfilling obligations. He places little emphasis on achieving results for their own sake and is likely to be motivated only by specific goals that mean something to him.

Daniel and the current situation: Unlike some of his colleagues, Daniel is quite content with the routine nature of the work, and he has not put himself forward for additional responsibility or developmental assignments. Outside work he spends much of his time writing reviews for various online publications, and this satisfies his need for intellectual stimulation without putting him under too much pressure to perform. It also supplements his income a bit and his needs are modest, so he is not as concerned as the others about the issue of pay and benefits. He is, however, very anxious about the security of his job and the risk that his skills will become less relevant in the coming years.

Overall, the risk for Daniel is that he lacks self-belief and under-values the contribution he could make even if the organization's requirements are quite different in future. At the moment he seems to be staying within his comfort zone, and this could have a negative impact on his resilience in the long term.

The Green Accounts team example shows how complex the inter-actions are between each person and the work situation they find themselves in. For reasons explained earlier, we have focused on personality traits as a guide to the personal resilience resources that individual team members bring to their work situation. A full account would, of course, need to include the coping strategies that each has learned to use over the years, as well as the more intellect-, experience- and knowledge-based capabilities that each possesses.

IMPLICATIONS FOR RESILIENCE-BUILDING

This discussion makes clear how important it is for everyone to understand (a) their personal resilience starting point and (b) how they are likely to be affected by the different types of pressure they face both at work and outside it. Managers and organizations also need to take account of these factors in order to support the personal development of others.

The interaction of individuals and their work context has a number of implications for resilience-building activities:

- If individuals evaluate just their personal resilience resources, without taking into account the effects of the context they work and live in, it will be much harder for them to play an active role in building their personal resilience.
- An understanding of the issues discussed in this chapter should help individuals and their managers to make the most of on-the-job opportunities for resilience-building—and to manage the workplace risks that have the potential to undermine personal resilience.

■ The design of workplace resilience-building programs and other interventions should take account of the different sources of pressure and support and the way these interact with individual traits and abilities. This is important for all such interventions, and critical for those that seek to achieve a broad, holistic approach to improving organizational well-being and performance.

It should also be clear from the account provided here that personal resilience will benefit from anything a person can do to build their *Confidence, Social Support* skills, *Adaptability* and *Purposefulness*. In Part 2 we do not attempt to list all the various techniques and training methods that relate to building these resources, as the span of this exercise would be far too broad. Instead, we set out general developmental principles that have particular relevance for improving resilience, and discuss in detail some of the most significant techniques and advances in the field.

CHAPTER 3

RESILIENCE-BUILDING OVER THE YEARS—FROM REMEDIAL TO PERFORMANCE-ENHANCING

Resilience development programs have appeared in various forms and contexts over the past twenty years, but despite consistently good results they have generally failed to take root and spread. Now, however, there are strong signs that this could change. Demand for *resilience training* (or "resiliency training") is higher than ever before. It seems that the value of personal development in general is now more widely accepted beyond the human resources and learning and development communities. It is also clear that economic and social pressures are having a major impact on the world of work. This has certainly been the case before, but today there is greater consensus that these pressures will continue to grow unrelentingly in future.

Nevertheless, in our view there is still work to be done to ensure that workplace resilience development is well-designed, widely adopted, and sustained over time—as it needs to be in order to deliver enduring results for individual employees and organizations alike. If this is an outcome you are interested in, then a good place to start is an understanding of what has happened in the field up to now.

JOB LOSS SUPPORT AND BACK-TO-WORK PROGRAMMES

As mentioned in the Introduction, there was surprisingly little take-up of resilience training in the private sector following the impressive results of the University of London training programs in the early 1990s. The approach did, however, gain more traction in sectors concerned with providing support to the unemployed and helping them to get back to work. This was a time when people in the UK were having to get used to the idea of mass redundancies, and the outplacement market was one of the few growth industries. Some providers of outplacement counseling introduced resilience training sessions as part of their support package, basing the design of these sessions on the University of London model.

In this context, reservations about psychological interventions were less of an issue, given the sector's use of counseling and related training interventions involving assertiveness and interpersonal skills. However, there were other barriers common to the financial services and outplacement sectors. In particular, the results achieved by the University of London studies were based on participants attending a half-day session every week for seven weeks (to allow time for real-life application and personal learning exercises). While the value of this approach was generally recognized, it presented many practical obstacles including issues of logistics and cost. As a result, elements of the model tended to be incorporated into existing training and one-to-one counseling interventions, and a wider roll-out of the full training program did not take place.

These days, many more counselors, trainers, and coaches are familiar with the principles of cognitive-behavioral psychology that lay at the heart of the University of London resilience training program. That was not the case in the early 1990s, which may have made it difficult to sustain personal resilience development as a core aspect of outplacement provision, even though the evidence for its effectiveness was overwhelming.

The evidence included significantly greater success for participants in finding work within four months of competing the training, when compared to a control group receiving a different kind of job-search training.[1] These results were naturally of considerable interest to the Employment Service, the government agency responsible for helping to increase levels of employment in the UK at the time. The Employment Service was involved in the University of London research study on resilience training, and did go on to implement further programs using the model.

Over the years, similar programs have been introduced by various government bodies in the UK and other countries, with the aim of improving the mental health of unemployed people and reducing unemployment. Progress has, however, been patchy and difficult to achieve. Based on an evaluation of the Australian experience, Vanessa Rose and Elizabeth Harris discuss the difficulties of sustaining large-scale, publicly funded interventions of this kind, beyond the context of research-based studies. They conclude that "Simply having the evidence for the efficacy of an intervention does not guarantee its effective dissemination to people who are unemployed."[2]

At the time of writing, the latest incarnation of government-funded support for resilience development in the UK is the inclusion of mental resilience in the skills training offered under the banner of the Youth Contract—a policy aimed specifically at reducing youth unemployment.

CAREER RESILIENCE

Related developments during the 1990s in the United States saw many companies, especially in the information technology sector, turn to the idea of "career resiliency" or "career resilience." This is defined as "the ability to manage one's career in a rapidly changing environment. The result of being career self-reliant... the ability to adapt to changing circumstances, even when the circumstances are discouraging or disruptive."[3]

The latter description shows how closely related the concept is to that of personal or individual resilience as we have defined it in this book. In practice, however, the idea was developed specifically to inform career development and career management procedures, in response to the changing nature of employment and what was seen as the demise of traditional, stable career paths and a "job for life." The idea was promoted by high-technology companies such as Sun Microsystems in California, who encouraged workers to see the industry, rather than specific organizations, as their employer. Organizational interventions were focused on developing a "Career Resilient Work Force—a group of career employees who not only are dedicated to the idea of continuous learning but also stand ready to reinvent themselves to keep pace with change, who take responsibility for their own career management, and last but not least, who are committed to the company's success."[4]

This was a successful and influential approach, although the wider roll-out was watered down and in some cases even compromised, by failure to understand and implement some of the most innovative and insightful specifics. A simplistic application of the approach could lead an organization to be criticized for washing its hands of responsibility for career development, whereas one of the core principles was to recognize the reality of the changing nature of employment, and invest in programs designed to help employees value and take responsibility for developing their "portable" skills and competencies.

For anyone particularly interested in the career development aspects of personal resilience, it is worth reviewing the career resilience literature, with an eye to identifying and possibly trying out some of the specific techniques used by Sun Microsystems and other Silicon Valley companies. A good place to start is the Harvard Business Review article "Toward a Career-Resilient Workforce."[5]

HISTORY OF STRESS AWARENESS AND STRESS MANAGEMENT IN ORGANIZATIONS

There is one industry within the private sector that has for many years adopted a more comprehensive approach to employee well-being, including mental well-being issues such as stress management and resilience. Perhaps understandably healthcare organizations in general, and the large pharmaceutical companies in particular, have always appeared to be less nervous than other companies about engaging with issues of mental as well as physical health. Indeed, from the perspective of company brand and reputation, many see holistic employee well-being interventions as a business priority.

In several cases, this has included providing employees with training to help develop their personal resilience. One example is the GlaxoSmithKline (GSK) Personal Resilience (PR) program, a three-and-a-half hour workshop offered by this global pharmaceutical giant to all its employees (about 99,000 worldwide). The GSK workshop has been described in a case study on the UK Department of Work and Pensions website as "incorporating energy management principles" and enabling "employees to engage their energy and to implement behaviors that create a healthy, positive and resilient person."[6]

More broadly, the healthcare sector has typically been prominent in surveys and studies of best practice in employee well-being. A detailed example is set out in a case study by Fikry Isaac and Scott Ratzen of Johnson & Johnson, USA—a company described by the authors as "the largest health care company in the world."[7]

Throughout this book we are careful to distinguish personal resilience from general psychological or mental well-being. We also make it clear that resilience development is just one element of a program to improve stress management and employee well-being in organizations. There are, however, very close inter-connections among all three—personal resilience, stress management, and general well-being.

It makes sense, therefore, to take time here to set personal resilience development in the context of wider stress management and organizational well-being initiatives, and we start by looking at how this field has developed within the healthcare sector. As the pressure from business mergers and other economic factors mounted during the 1990s, the employee health departments of companies such as Glaxo, Wellcome, and their competitors began to focus on stress awareness and stress management. This was primarily a risk management approach driven by the occupational health function, so differed in emphasis and organizational ownership from the University of London studies which targeted specific outcomes for individuals (re-employment) and businesses (sales, retention etc.).

To start with, both research and practice focused mainly on reducing levels of stress in individual employees—a strategy in which personal resilience training played its part. There was, however, a growing recognition of the limitations of this approach. Researchers such as Cary Cooper and Susan Cartwright,[8] Cary Cooper and Sydney Finklestein[9] and Jac van der Klink[10] argued that the problem needed to be addressed on a more strategic level by identifying and managing the sources of stress within the employing organization.

By 2002, when the UK Health and Safety Executive (HSE) commissioned a study of best practice in stress management, organizations in the healthcare sector had begun to introduce a much wider range of interventions. The study, known as the "Beacons of Excellence" project,[11] confirmed the dominance of the multinational pharmaceutical companies among the private sector organizations prepared to invest in the mental health of their employees. It also revealed a widespread commitment to the issue among public sector organizations, with several councils and National Health Service (NHS) trusts judged to be "Beacons of Excellence" in terms of stress risk assessment, stress prevention strategy, and primary level interventions (tackling the root causes of workplace stress).

Among those organizations willing to invest in improving stress management, the idea of assessing and addressing organizational sources of stress had now taken hold. Together with academic researchers and public bodies such as the HSE, and through participation in projects such as the "Beacons of Excellence," these organizations helped to create a shared understanding of "what good looks like" in assessing and managing risks of workplace stress. Central to this was the definition of three distinct levels of stress management intervention: the primary, secondary, and tertiary levels described (see box).

Levels of stress management intervention:

■ Primary level: aimed at eradicating the stressor/s from the work environment, or at least reducing employees' exposure to the source of negative pressure (also known as a "hindrance" pressure). Likely to involve changes to strategy, policy, structures, procedures, or processes.

■ Secondary level: aimed at improving employees' ability to manage sources of workplace stress, especially those sources of stress that are difficult to address through primary interventions. Often involves personal development interventions such as training or coaching.

■ Tertiary level: aimed at helping individual employees to recover from the ill effects of stress or strain through work-related or more general life pressures. Typically involves some form of individual counseling, often through an external provider in the form of an "employee assistance programme" (EAP).

Workplace resilience training courses fall within the secondary level of stress management intervention. This suggests that although such courses do not aim to address the primary organizational sources of stress, they have an important role to play. In practice, however, they may be seen by employees as a "sticking plaster" to cover over the underlying problems, and indeed there is a risk of them being used this way by some organizations. The solution is to ensure that resilience training is just one element of a comprehensive and well-communicated well-being strategy, and in later chapters we discuss how this may be achieved.

Without this wider organizational framework in place, it can be very frustrating for individual leaders who recognize the value of resilience training and seek with the best of intentions to introduce it to their area of the business. In one such project we were involved with, the divisional head of a large organizational change function in the financial services industry commissioned a series of resilience training workshops. The workshops were part of a multi-faceted approach designed to support the leadership team and the wider employee group through a particularly tough set of challenges, given the central role they were playing in a major business integration and restructuring exercise.

Although the overall evaluation of the pilot workshops was positive, and although there was clear communication about other actions taken by the leadership team to iron out pressures caused by unnecessary demands and inefficient work practices, the roll-out stalled. The head of the division attributed this outcome to a perception that the workshops were a manipulative attempt to avoid addressing the real problems faced by employees. He understood that this was a risk but was surprised and disappointed by how widespread the cynicism was, given the leadership team's commitment to supporting the division's employees in a number of different ways.

Such experiences are by no means uncommon, and over the years senior managers have typically been reluctant to take the risk even when they are personally persuaded of the potential benefits. There has also been little pressure from other quarters to introduce programs to help employees develop their personal resilience. In the evolution of workplace well-being interventions, it is understandable that academics and bodies representing employee interests have spent the past decade emphasizing the need for primary level interventions. During the 1990s, tertiary interventions had become widely accepted and well established, while the need for organizational commitment to primary level interventions was becoming ever more pressing as organizations faced escalating external economic and environmental pressures.

As a result, those organizations committed to adopting best practices in stress management have tended to focus on assessing the risks of stress and developing follow-up action plans. In the UK, online stress auditing tools were introduced by the HSE and a small number of commercial providers. Most annual employee surveys also incorporated a few items designed to alert the organization to some of the most common causes of stress. Within the private sector, the general practice has been to rely on the annual employee survey to flag up systemic risks of stress, while taking specific action at the team or individual level in a reactive basis. Within the public and the commercial healthcare sectors the routine auditing of organizational sources of pressure became

78

more widespread, although by no means universal. For some this has changed again as public sector budgets are cut and employee surveys are centralized, along with the provision of training, development and related interventions.[12]

For public sector organizations operating under such restrictions, there is little scope for thorough stress risk assessments or for the bespoke interventions that follow to manage the sources of workplace pressure. This is despite the UK Government's own recommendations, in the form of the report of the Foresight Project on Mental Capital and Well-Being,[13] which emphasize the importance of carrying out regular organizational audits of well-being and sources of stress.

At the same time, however, in the wider organizational landscape there has been a surge of interest in employee well-being that extends beyond physical well-being or "wellness" to cover issues of morale and mental health. For some organizations this has taken the form of broadening their stress management interventions to accommodate other aspects of employee well-being. For many others, however, it is the first time that they have taken a strategic, organization-wide approach to issues affecting the mental health of their employees.

There are a number of drivers behind the current interest in employee well-being, but undoubtedly one of the most significant is the recognition that challenging economic and environmental conditions are here to stay. Over the past few years, we have observed two main avenues through which organizations tend to arrive at the conclusion that more needs to be done to sustain the mental health of their employees.

The first avenue is that of *employee engagement*, described by David MacLeod and Nita Clarke as "a workplace approach designed to ensure that employees are committed to their organization's goals and values, motivated to contribute to organizational success, and are able at the same time to enhance their own sense of well-being."[14] Interest in measuring employee engagement has expanded to the point where many annual employee surveys have been rebranded "engagement surveys." For many, the business case for investing in improving employee engagement has been made, and this acceptance appears to have paved the way for a greater focus on employees' morale and mental health.

Another group of organizations has homed in specifically on the *high levels of pressure* that many employees need to cope with *as a result of tough economic circumstances and the rapid pace of change.* A few companies, such as Questar in the US, introduced organization-wide employee resilience-training programs in the late 1990s, in response to the growing pace of change and anxieties about "Y2K" (the anticipated technology-related problems of the turn of the century). They were, however, very much in the minority.

NEW INTEREST IN THE DEVELOPMENT OF PERSONAL RESILIENCE

More widespread interest began to build during the international financial crisis of 2008, with requests for resilience training coming from organizations previously considered to have a rather dismissive or "macho" attitude to pressure in the workplace. It is not clear whether such initiatives would have spread much beyond a relatively small number of organizations at the centre of the financial crisis, if it were not for growing publicity for the master resiliency training component of the US Army's Comprehensive Soldier Fitness program, launched in 2009. This program, developed in collaboration with the University of Pennsylvania, is designed to improve five dimensions of personal strength—described as the *emotional*, *social*, *spiritual*, *family*, and *physical* dimensions.

One of the main contributors to the design of the master resilience-training was Professor Martin Seligman, whose early work in the field provided a foundation for the University of London programs described at the beginning of this chapter. The approach applied to the US Army program has much in common with this early work, but it has also been significantly adapted and developed to incorporate recent theory and research—particularly in the field of positive psychology. A more detailed account of the master resiliency training is provided in later chapters.

Even within the context of the unquestionable stress faced by soldiers deployed to Afghanistan and other conflict-affected regions, resilience training is by no means a universally accepted intervention. In the case of the US Army training, some commentators are critical of various aspects of the program and the way it has been implemented. Whatever perspective one takes on their specific arguments, it should probably be viewed as a good thing for any resilience development intervention to be subjected to close scrutiny and challenge. These are, after all, interventions that aim to shape the way we think about and respond to significant events, both at work and more generally in our everyday lives.

MATURING OF THE WORKPLACE WELL-BEING AGENDA—IMPLICATIONS FOR RESILIENCE DEVELOPMENT

This observation brings us back to the need for personal resilience development to be incorporated into strategic well-being programs that are properly designed and communicated, and that have the support of senior management and other stakeholder groups. This is what we believe needs to happen to achieve sustainability and results for the organization over time, and it requires more than a comprehensive set of interventions put in place by the occupational health department.

Although it is still early days, a growing number of organizations are putting together a well-being strategy that is driven by the senior leadership team and owned by stakeholders in functions as diverse as corporate social responsibility, talent management, customer services, risk and compliance, and health and safety. To illustrate, in the case of the company Johnson & Johnson, future plans extend beyond traditional employee healthcare goals to outcomes related to the company's environmental and social impact, and to incorporating better measures of employee performance, satisfaction, and engagement as well as linking well-being initiatives to company profitability.[15]

This extension of interest and ownership beyond the traditional boundaries of the human resources function owes much to recent evidence for a variety of business benefits associated with improved employee well-being. We have already mentioned long-standing evidence for the specific benefits of developing personal resilience, such as increased sales and retention. Effective stress management has also been clearly linked for some time to reduced costs and to better employee attendance and retention. Over the past decade, however, a growing body of research has demonstrated the impact that employee well-being can have on many different hard measures of business success. These measures include customer satisfaction and a range of productivity indicators associated with organizational performance and profitability.

The business case for improving employee well-being—illustrative findings:

- Almost a quarter (23%) of variance in employee productivity (as reported by a sample of 16,000 UK employees) is explained by:
  - psychological well-being;
  - perceived commitment of organization to employee;
  - resources and communications.[16]
- A five-year longitudinal study of psychological well-being and performance found a strong correlation between well-being and work performance.[17]
- Data from nearly 8,000 separate business units in 36 companies showed engagement and well-being to be correlated with business unit performance (sickness-absence, customer satisfaction, productivity, employee turnover, etc.).[18]
- Developing confidence, hope, optimism, and resilience has been found to improve individual and organizational performance.[19]

Clearly, senior leaders who wish to take advantage of these benefits must be prepared to audit levels of employee well-being and take action to address any risks identified. Such actions may be described as primary interventions, based on the stress management framework described earlier. So how do secondary interventions fit with this new, strategic approach to well-being? As the study on confidence, hope, and optimism mentioned above shows, improving personal resilience and related characteristics such as confidence can lead directly to better organizational performance.

This brings us back, however, to the concern that some organizations see developing personal resilience as a "quick-fix" option that delivers the business benefits of employee well-being without the challenges and costs of identifying and addressing underlying problems in organizational culture, systems, or processes. The limitations of such an approach are particularly marked in cases where short resilience training workshops of two hours or less are rolled out across the organization using a "one-hit" model without opportunity for practice, follow-up, and embedding of the learning from the workshop.

In our experience, there is a particular challenge for Human Resource and Healthcare professionals in ensuring that resilience development provision is well designed and effective. As more senior leadership teams come to appreciate the strategic business benefits of investing in well-being and resilience, so the pressure increases for the organization's professionals to source high impact, cost-effective solutions. Unfortunately, high impact does not always necessarily translate into long-lasting benefit for individual participants or for the organization—especially in the case of developing personal resilience. As long as this problem is recognized and avoided, resilience development and other secondary interventions should be able to take their place and play an important role in an organization's employee well-being program.

THE WAY FORWARD: INTEGRATING RESILIENCE DEVELOPMENT WITH BROADER INTERVENTIONS

From the preceding overview of how things have evolved over the past twenty years, it can be seen that it is not the norm for resilience training to be an integral part of a wider, strategic program, but there is potential for this to change. What, then, needs to happen to ensure that such integration is standard practice going forward? One of the first steps is *to provide a framework that clearly locates resilience within the broader context of well-being and performance.*

We have defined personal resilience as the ability to keep going in difficult circumstances and to recover from stressful events in a way that strengthens our coping skills and provides enduring benefits. We have also shown how some organizations have incorporated resilience training into their stress management programs. In this context, *primary interventions* are those that remove or alleviate the sources of workplace pressure, *tertiary interventions* help people recover when their health has been adversely affected by pressure, while *secondary interventions* like resilience training equip employees to cope with pressure so that they stand a better chance of avoiding burnout and ill-health.

Clearly, pressure is a core concept linking resilience development with other aspects of stress management. In fact, it is also one of the fundamental links between resilience and workplace well-being in general, although this may seem less obvious at first. Pressure in the workplace has typically been viewed in a negative light—something to be avoided if the risks of stress and burn-out are to be managed. Leaders and managers have been aware of the need to set high expectations and to encourage effort and performance, but only in more specific circumstances are they likely to describe this as putting people under pressure. In recent years, however, the study of psychology has drawn our attention to the way *challenge pressure* of this kind can be *a positive force for well-being*—an essential ingredient in fact.

The idea of "challenge pressure" as central to well-being is not a new one in the study of philosophy. Early Greek philosophers distinguished between two views of well-being. The *hedonic* view defines well-being purely in terms of pleasure—giving rise to the term "hedonistic." The *eudaimonic* view, on the other hand, argues that pleasure and happiness are insufficient on their own, and that true well-being is experienced only when people are engaged with pursuing meaningful goals and have an opportunity to realize their potential.

The latter view—the "eudaimonic approach"—is now taking hold in the study and practice of psychology, where it is central to the field known as positive psychology. This discipline is described as follows by the Positive Psychology Center at the University of Pennsylvania:

> the scientific study of the strengths and virtues that enable individuals and communities to thrive.... This field is founded on the belief that people want to lead meaningful and fulfilling lives, to cultivate what is best within themselves, and to enhance their experiences of love, work, and play.[20]

In exploring what it takes to achieve a meaningful life, positive psychology places great emphasis on the need for a sense of purpose. An easy life is not necessarily seen as ideal and tough challenges can play an important and beneficial role in personal well-being.

This is consistent with recent research findings in the field of work-related stress, which demonstrate how the right type and amount of pressure can benefit general well-being and performance, as well as helping us to build our resilience for the future. For many years, research-based models of stress have recognized the possibility that insufficient pressure may be as damaging to performance as too much pressure, although far more attention has been paid to the latter risk. As long ago as 1908, the Yerkes–Dodson principle suggested that low levels of arousal may be associated with poor task performance. This

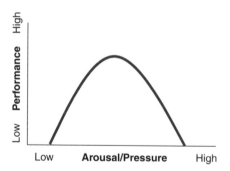

FIGURE 3.1   **Common representation of the Yerkes–Dodson law**

idea, represented by the Yerkes–Dodson law (Figure 3.1), became widely popular in the 1950s as a way of representing the relationship between arousal (or pressure) and performance.

Since then the "inverted U hypothesis" has been challenged by many researchers.[21] Their findings have not generally supported the smooth curve or the explanations typically associated with the inverted U shown in Figure 3.1. However, as mentioned above, there is good evidence from other studies to show that in principle too much and too little pressure both have a negative effect on well-being and work performance, even if this does not work in the way suggested by the Yerkes–Dodson law.

The negative effects of too much pressure on well-being and performance have been well documented in the literature on work-place stress for many years.[22] More recently, investigators seeking to reduce the human and economic costs of work stress have turned up some interesting findings that shine a light on the issue of too little pressure as well. In one influential study reported in 2000, Maureen Dollard and her colleagues[23] explored the impact of certain conditions in the work environment on employee stress. They looked at three main factors—(i) the level of demand placed on employees (pressure of work and time urgency), (ii) the level of support they received (from colleagues and managers), and (iii) the level of control or autonomy they had at work (the extent to which employees were encouraged to be self-sufficient and make their own decisions).

Unsurprisingly, they found that conditions of "high demand combined with low support and low control" led to the lowest levels of employee satisfaction. "High demand and low support" led

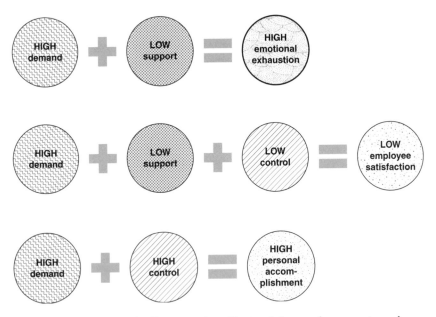

FIGURE 3.2   **Main findings on the effects of demand, support, and control (autonomy), Dollard et al. 2000**

to negative outcomes including high levels of emotional exhaustion. However, high demand was not a bad thing under all circumstances—where demand and control (autonomy) were both high, employees reported the highest levels of personal accomplishment (feelings of productivity and competency). This suggests that low levels of demand (pressure) may detract from our ability to feel and perform at our best. It also helps explain a common finding in organizational stress risk assessments, where senior managers report lower levels of strain than junior members of staff even though they may be troubled by workload pressures and lack of work–life balance. For them, high demand (pressure) feels challenging but manageable because they also have a high degree of control over their work and the decisions that affect them.

Another group of researchers[24] separated work demands into two categories, labeled "challenge" and "hindrance" stressors (sources of pressure). "Challenge demands" included *high workload, time pressure, high levels of responsibility,* and *a broad job scope.* They referred to these as challenge stressors because people viewed them as obstacles to be overcome in order to learn and achieve. "Hindrance demands" included *organizational politics, bureaucracy, role ambiguity,* and *concerns about job security*—demands that were seen as unnecessary barriers to personal growth and the achievement of goals. In a series of studies, these researchers found that both types of demand were stressors that could, under certain circumstances, cause employees to suffer strain (e.g. anxiety, exhaustion, or burn-out). However, challenge demands had a largely positive relationship with motivation and performance, while hindrance demands had a negative relationship with performance.

As can be seen from the detail of these studies, the popular concept of "good stress" and "bad stress" is probably too simplistic, although it is intuitively appealing. Nevertheless, it is safe to conclude that *there are conditions under which workplace pressures can have a positive impact on well-being and performance, while under other conditions the impact is a negative one.* Clearly the goal should not be to minimize or remove pressure altogether from the work environment. Instead it should be to facilitate the active and well-informed management of the different sources of pressure, by individual employees and managers, and by the organization as a whole. The first goal is implicit in many stress management approaches, while the second is consistent with the more rounded well-being approaches that are now being adopted by forward-thinking organizations.

We have shown how the active management of pressure is central, not only to resilience and stress risk management, but also to the broad, strategic relationship between employee well-being and performance. This provides the foundation for an approach that enables us to set resilience within the context of employee well-being and performance. We see this approach less as a theoretical or research model, and more as a practical organizing framework for understanding, assessing, and managing pressure in the workplace, with the overall objective of improving employee well-being and organizational performance.

THE ACTIVE MANAGEMENT OF PRESSURE AT WORK

We first applied the concept of "keeping pressure positive" around 2005, as we looked for ways of helping clients to address the leadership issues that typically emerged, in one form or another, from the results of their organizational stress and well-being audits. Around this time, we found that senior leaders were becoming more engaged with the results of these audits, and increasingly willing to take on board the need for action on issues of leadership style and organizational culture. Their question to us was "okay then, so what do we do about it." While these leaders had typically been exposed to various leadership frameworks, and were very familiar with different approaches to organizational change and development, the question was how to integrate leadership best practice with knowledge and insights from the fields of stress management and employee well-being.

Taking the idea of "challenge versus hindrance pressure" into the leadership arena, it becomes evident that leaders and managers need to play a role in ensuring that *workplace pressure is reasonable, positive, and motivating rather than unreasonable, damaging, and de-motivating.* "Intrinsic motivation" is said to be highest when a goal is seen to be stretching but possibly achievable, and leaders can help to create these conditions by providing a balance of challenge and support.[25]

Within the traditional stress management approach, the emphasis was generally on ensuring that leaders and managers provided the necessary support. As a more strategic focus on well-being and performance gained ground, we considered the idea of a balance between challenge and support to be more useful and relevant. Certainly it was more appealing to leaders, who often worry that the demands of stress management and well-being initiatives will conflict with their responsibility for setting high standards and meeting the organization's performance targets.

With these observations in mind, we developed the "Leadership Impact" approach[26] to help leaders (a) evaluate and adjust their own impact on levels of well-being among those who report to them and (b) understand and actively manage the sources of pressure in the work environments for which they were responsible. From the outset, we incorporated a personal resilience development component for the leaders, on the basis that it is difficult to have a positive impact on the well-being of others if your own coping strategies are reaching their limit. We also developed a leadership profiling tool to help people in leadership roles evaluate their likely impact on others' well-being, based on our research linking personality and leadership style with each of the six main sources of workplace pressure.

Central to all this is the idea that leaders need to manage their own impact, as well as other factors under their control, in such a way as to achieve a balance between challenge and support for

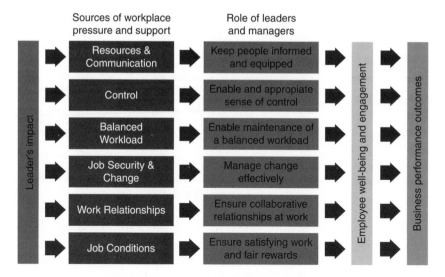

FIGURE 3.3 **Flow chart showing the direction of the impact of leader's personality on well-being and performance outcomes (through the six main sources of workplace pressure and support)**

those who report to them. The responsibility of individual leaders and of leadership teams is to "keep pressure positive" for employees as well as for themselves. In this endeavor, one of the most important risks for leaders to manage is that of over-using their personal strengths.[27] In other words, a drive for results is a great leadership characteristic, but if taken to extreme, it can have a negative impact on employees' well-being (and on organizational performance). Similarly, self-confidence has many benefits for a leader's influence and effectiveness, but being over-confident can easily result in negative consequences for both leader and team.

This work linking leadership style and employee well-being set the foundation for the new approach to assessing personal resilience described in Chapters 1 and 2. In our leadership impact research studies, we investigated the predictive relationship between leader personality (or "natural style") on the one hand, and levels of well-being among those who report to them, on the other. In measuring levels of employee well-being we used a version of the research-based ASSET model that assesses six main sources of workplace pressure: Work Relationships, Workload and Work Life Balance, Control, Resources and Communication, Job Security and Change, and Sense of Purpose.

Main sources of pressure and support in the workplace - example	Positive pressures bringing us up the pressure/performance curve	Support helping to keep us at the top of the curve	Negative pressures pushing us over the top into burn-out
Work relationships Optimum for well-being and performance: relationships constructive and collaborative but also stimulating/challenging	e.g. constructive debate and/or healthy competition within the team	e.g. colleagues sharing the workload when someone is absent; sharing expertise	e.g. aggressive management style; others taking credit for your achievements, isolation and/or lack of support from others

FIGURE 3.4   **The ASSET factors as sources of workplace pressure and support—example Work Relationships**

This gave us a framework which incorporated a well-validated theoretical model of the individual (the FFM, see Chapter 1) with a model of the situation (the six main sources of workplace pressure, from the ASSET model). As we developed and researched this framework further, we recognized that the six factors listed above could potentially be sources of support, as well as sources of positive or negative pressure (see example in Figure 3.4, and Chapter 2 for a more detailed discussion). Leaders and managers who learned to understand, assess, and manage these six workplace factors were in a much stronger position to achieve a good balance between challenge and support for their teams.

Personality profiling is a widely used tool in the assessment and development practices of organizations, but it is rarely combined with a valid, theoretical model of the workplace situation—especially with employee well-being as the outcome of interest. The benefits that emerged from our leadership and well-being work encouraged us to develop a similar approach for the assessment of individual or personal resilience. Instead of predicting how a leader's personality was likely to impact on the well-being of others, this approach uses the same theoretical models (the Five-Factor Model of personality and the ASSET model of workplace well-being) to explore how personality affects the way people cope with typical workplace stressors. This formed the basis for the *i-resilience* report and for the individual–work situation framework described in Chapters 1 and 2.

PUTTING RESILIENCE-BUILDING IN ITS PLACE

From the discussion above it can be seen that specific, isolated resilience-building interventions (such as a one-off, half-day course) are a limited way of approaching the issue in your organization, although in some cases they may be a good way to begin. Much more is to be gained by considering how resilience development can best be integrated into a broader program of leadership, well-being, and organizational performance improvement. This approach is discussed in Part 3.

Many organizations have used the online ASSET survey tool to take stock of the current sources of workplace pressure and support. Given its history in organizational stress management, the ASSET tool is well suited for use in a context where resilience development is part of the overall intervention. Another tool that has its roots more in the recent positive psychology and happiness movement is the Happiness at Work survey, launched in 2012 by Nef Consulting at the New Economics Foundation. This online survey is designed to provide real-time feedback to employees, teams, and managers on well-being in the workplace. As with ASSET, the questions reflect what the evidence says impacts on well-being at work and the reporting provides national benchmarks.

Results for the Happiness at Work survey are presented in the form of a Happiness Landscape made up of the following categories: Our People, Our People at Work, Our Jobs, Our Relationships, Our Organization, and Social Impact. Underpinning the survey is a dynamic model, reflecting the dynamic and interconnected nature of people's working lives. This is represented in an alternative view of the results, summarizing how the respondents' "experience of work" (how they feel) is influenced by how they are "functioning at work" (what they do)...which in turn is dependent on both the "organizational system" they work in (where they work) and their personal resources (who they are).

Engagement and general staff surveys may also include items that provide useful insights for an integrated program of well-being and performance improvement. Great care should be taken, however, to avoid relying too heavily on these broad surveys. In many cases even those sections that are labeled "well-being" fail to get at how people are actually feeling—tapping instead into views and opinions on specific organizational activities that have been selected as having particular current relevance to the organization's objectives.

An integrated program of well-being and organizational performance improvement should always include a robust measure of current levels of well-being (as well as indicators of organizational performance). As we have made very clear, high levels of well-being do not equate to high levels of personal resilience. Nevertheless, a careful analysis of the well-being results can be used to support the resilience-building element of the program in a number of ways, as discussed in Chapters 2 and in Part 2.

PART 2

BUILDING RESILIENCE

CHAPTER 4

WHAT INDIVIDUALS CAN DO TO BUILD THEIR RESILIENCE

There is much that people managers and organizations can do to support and sustain individual resilience, as we shall see in later chapters. Ultimately, however, every person has a unique pattern of resilience that they have built up over the years, and that they bring with them into all situations, including work. Building resilience is, therefore, primarily an individual endeavor for which everyone needs to take personal responsibility. Those who succeed in raising their resilience to the next level will experience enduring benefits in all aspects of their lives.

In this chapter and the next, we set out a range of principles and techniques that apply to resilience-building in any context. These approaches are not specific to the workplace, but they do provide the foundation for resilience training, and other forms of support offered by employing organizations. Here we describe actions individuals can take to build their personal resilience levels. Some of these actions are aimed specifically and directly at building resilience, while others have a more general application and affect resilience in an indirect way. In Chapters 6 and 7, we discuss in more detail how individual resilience development can be supported by managers and organizations.

Considering the many factors—genes, life experiences, personality, etc.—that shape personal resilience in the first place, it is easy to see why there is no single approach or solution to improving it. A multi-faceted construct like resilience requires a multi-faceted approach. The contributing factors are highly interdependent, each one feeding the others—hence our emphasis on both direct and indirect influences on resilience, and on the complex and interactive relationship between resilience and well-being.

As you read through the techniques and illustrations in this chapter and the next, we invite you to think about your own situation and try the exercises out for yourself. This will give you a good foundation for supporting others' resilience development, as well as providing you with the opportunity to raise your own resilience to the next level.

TACKLING THE PERSONAL CHALLENGE OF DEVELOPING RESILIENCE

The usefulness and relevance of the different approaches described below will vary depending on each person's unique make-up, experience, and circumstances. It is worth noting, however, that it is always important to tackle resilience-building from more than one angle, and to address both psychological and physical aspects in order to gain the maximum benefit. Similarly, building resilience within the context of a work role can bring definite benefits, but it is important to remember that individual resilience affects and reflects the whole of one's life. Treating resilience development as an activity confined to the context of a work role will have limited benefit.

The first important step is to recognize that every person has it in his or her power to improve personal resilience. It may not be easy, but only the individual concerned has the necessary control to apply core resilience-building techniques such as "challenging unhelpful assumptions," "adapting behavior," and "learning new coping skills." Only they can fully understand the current starting point, work out how to make the most of their personal resilience strengths, and develop additional coping skills and strategies to manage their resilience risks. To achieve this each person needs to (i) analyze what form his or her own resilience takes, (ii) identify which actions will be most helpful in boosting resilience, and (iii) make a development plan that has a reasonable chance of being implemented. If you are seeking to provide resilience-building support for others, you will need to think about how to get this message across.

We saw earlier that resilience has four main components: *Confidence*, *Social Support*, *Adaptability*, and *Purposefulness*. We will address each of these in turn in the next chapter. First, in this chapter, we look at:

- the potential benefits of building resilience;
- the first step: understanding your personal starting point;

■ two of the most important developmental techniques—broad approaches that apply to building all four components of resilience.

POTENTIAL BENEFITS OF BUILDING PERSONAL RESILIENCE

When groups of workers (at any level or any function within an organization) are asked what might be the potential benefits of building personal resilience to their work lives, typical responses include greater openness to change, better team working, improved communications, feeling more motivated, less cynicism, feeling more engaged, and less stress. When asked how increased resilience could benefit their lives as whole, typical answers include more energy, more time for my friends, better relationships, coping with stress, feel better in myself, life not just a treadmill, more optimistic, and readier to experiment and try new things. For these workers, there is considerable overlap in the hoped-for benefits in their work lives and their lives as a whole.

UNDERSTANDING YOUR PERSONAL STARTING POINT

In Chapter 1, we set out a framework for understanding personal resilience strengths and risks, in which we provided an overview of theory and research into the various definitions, determinants, and underlying characteristics of resilience. In Chapter 2 we emphasized the importance of understanding how individual resilience factors—in particular the traits described by the Five-Factor Model (FFM) of personality—interact with situational factors, described in terms of the main sources of workplace pressure and support (the ASSET framework).

Having set this out from a theoretical and research-based perspective, we come now to the practical application of this approach. For each person this involves (i) using the FFM (in addition to more resilience-specific measures) as an organizing framework to understand their personal resilience strengths and risks, (ii) using the ASSET framework to understand the main sources of pressure and support in the work environment, and (iii) applying this understanding to work out which work pressures they are best equipped to deal with, and which are likely to cause them the most stress. This analysis will make it possible to select the most useful resilience-building approaches for each person's needs, and will ensure they benefit from the energy and effort they invest in these developmental activities.

As indicated above, resilience-building is not restricted to the work context, so the principle of working out one's personal vulnerability to specific situational pressures can be applied to other contexts as well. The benefit lies in understanding that people are not equally vulnerable or resilient towards all sources of pressure. So in order to improve their resilience, each person needs to understand which pressures are likely to affect them most—problems with relationships, problems with control and influence, problems with changing circumstances, and so on. Recognizing that one is most at risk when things go wrong with relationships, for example, is an important first step in taking action to develop coping strategies that will help in pre-empting or recovering from problems of this nature.

Figure 1.7 provides a general guide to assessing personal strengths and risks in relation to the four main components of resilience—the resilience resources. For this purpose, you could make use of any sound, well-established tool that assesses the characteristics listed in this figure (self-control, sociability etc.), supplemented perhaps by 360° feedback and other observations of current style and behavior. For a comprehensive assessment fully aligned with the approach described in this book, you could use a combination of the personality-based *i-resilience* measure[1] and the Ashridge Resilience Questionnaire (ARQ), which directly measures current resilient attitudes (see Chapter 2 for details). Referring back to Chapters 1 and 2 of this book will provide guidance on relating personal profiles to the main sources of pressure at work, and on making the best use of such assessments to inform personal resilience development planning and activities. Each person will need to consider which of their character strengths (e.g. conscientiousness, enthusiasm etc.) are most likely to turn into resilience risks if they over-use them, and to think about how they can flex their style to manage these risks.

GETTING THINGS IN PERSPECTIVE—THE FIRST BROAD APPROACH TO RESILIENCE-BUILDING

In this section we describe an approach that has for many years provided the main foundation for clinical treatments for anxiety and depression, and that has been adapted to suit workplace resilience training programs. This is the cognitive approach, also often referred to as "re-framing." In essence it involves (i) identifying underlying beliefs and assumptions, (ii) checking them to see how realistic and helpful they are, and (iii) adjusting them to ensure that things are being seen in the most positive and realistic light. We describe it here as a *broad approach* because it encompasses a number of specific techniques, and because its application is of great importance for both *Confidence* and *Adaptability*, and can also help boost *Social Support* and *Purposefulness*. In other words, it is a powerful method for developing all four main components of personal resilience.

The benefits of a positive mindset

As we saw earlier, how you think about an event influences how you feel, and how you feel influences the actions you are likely to take. A famous series of studies at Stanford University used the classic Prisoner's Dilemma game to study the power of thinking over individuals' interpretation of the world. It is a game in which if one cheats and lies one stands to win everything, while if no-one cheats both sides gain but to a lesser extent. Experiments revealed that when it was called a Community Game virtually no-one cheated, but when it was called the Wall Street Game, everyone cheated, because they were afraid of what the other players would do and did not trust what they said[2]—same game, different mindset.

Psychologists have been studying and deepening our understanding of this phenomenon for many decades. It goes under many names but perhaps the best way to capture it is MINDSET. In short, positive thinking habits help to maintain a sense of well-being and strengthen resilience. Large amounts of research reveal clearly that happier people with a positive outlook (i) are less prone to critical self-reflection (rumination), (ii) avoid negative social comparisons with others, and (iii) tend to interpret events positively rather than negatively.[3] In short they have positive mindsets. These people also tend to be more successful in their careers, have more positive relationships, be healthier, and live longer.

The benefits from a positive outlook are far-reaching, both in people's work lives and in their lives as a whole. These benefits can range from lower turnover at work, better customer service and increased sales, to higher job satisfaction, more inclusive thinking toward others, increased motivation, and better decision-making efficiency.

Developing a positive mindset

The good news is that one can learn to see and interpret the world in a more positive light. This is not to say that if you want something enough and truly believe in yourself, you can make anything happen. This idea is very seductive but only partially true. The other contributing factors that advocates of such simplistic positive thinking neglect to emphasize are the critical roles played by talent, opportunity, encouragement, focus, hard work, resilience, and luck.

It is true, however, that if you expect to fail the chances of failure are increased. If you expect to succeed, the chances of success might be increased. The glittering prizes dangled by the positive thinking industry (based on sales of videos, CDs, mobile apps, books, and motivational talks) come to only a few. For many, the unbridled belief in the magic formula of positive thinking can create unrealistic expectations, followed by disappointment and sometimes despair. Relentless and unrealistic positive thinking can be bad for one's health, just as obsessive negative thinking can undermine individual effectiveness. The challenge lies in finding skills and techniques that help maintain a healthier and productive balance between the extremes of unhelpful negative thinking and naïve positive thinking.

As we have seen, expectations, habits of thinking, and assumptions have powerful effects on our behavior and thoughts. People who habitually see "problems as threats" undermine their resilience, in part because their bodies are continuously experiencing the hormones (adrenaline and cortisol, among others) associated with stress and negative emotions. Their bodies are on constant alert, ready to deal with perceived and actual threats. At an extreme this can interfere with the immune system and undermine health. It can also undermine performance at work.

By contrast, an achievable challenge is seen as a potential source of satisfaction, and as a result different hormones (such as dopamine and other feel good hormones) race through the body. These are pleasure hormones that underlie positive emotions and that encourage enthusiasm, openness, curiosity, and perseverance.

It is worth remembering that your body can be in a state of high alert or physiological arousal without your being fully aware of this. For sustained periods this can have serious effects on health and the efficiency of the immune system.

The lens of Stress, Negativity and Uncertainty

The lens of Resilience, Positivity and Optimism

FIGURE 4.1   **Positive and negative lenses**

So, how can the idea of mindset be used to take control of this situation and improve resilience? Broadly speaking, one can look at the world in two ways. Persistent negative thinking often has a pattern of negative consequences that can be self-fulfilling, and as a result the negativity increases. People are often trapped by their automatic thoughts in response to a situation—thoughts that make them feel worse and less able to cope.

Here is a brief list of common automatic negative thoughts and likely consequences, together with alternative more positive ways of thinking about the same situation. It is possible to learn to recognize automatic negative thoughts and supplant them with more constructive thoughts, as we describe later in this chapter.

Automatic reaction	Consequence	Alternative
I will never get over this	Take longer to recover	People always recover; it just takes time
There is no point trying	Won't even try to do something about it	There is always a way
It will never be the same again	Resist or fight change	There is good in every situation
I will never get promoted	Less likely to try	Must find out what I need to do to get promoted
The Sales Department never listens to us	They sense your negativity and don't want to cooperate	Let's see whether we can understand why. What can we do to help them?

Be an agent not a victim

When faced with problems or setbacks, some people get emotional and feel sorry for themselves, while others face problems and take

101

action to deal with them. The "victim mentality" can be a dangerous downward spiral. Things only feel worse and make the individual feel even less able to cope. The "agent mentality" can be hard, but the confidence that things will change over time, and that taking action makes a difference, results in less vulnerability to self-pity, passivity, and anger. Not everything is under your control but to the extent that it is, you can make choices about, and work hard at, adopting a positive rather than negative mindset.

It is normal and healthy to feel upset or angered by problems and setbacks. These feelings help you to recognize a problem and motivate you to take action. The challenge lies in getting out of anger and self-pity quickly so that *appropriate* action can be taken. There are people who live under stressful and demanding conditions but who rarely get sick or become depressed. These people tend to feel in control, are committed to what they do (work, family, self), and see challenges they can deal with rather feeling beset with insuperable problems.

Four related variations of the cognitive approach to changing mindset and building resilience are:

1. increasing optimism;
2. re-framing problems;
3. becoming a merit-finder;
4. recognizing and avoiding thinking traps (automatic negative thoughts).

1. *Increasing optimism*

The overarching quality possessed by resilient people is an optimistic outlook. "Optimists" tend to see their problems as short-lived, changeable, and specific to circumstances. By contrast, "dispositional or habitual pessimists" see their problems as permanent, persistent, and pervasive. Pessimists tend to blame themselves for setbacks and failures, whereas optimists tend to look elsewhere for the reasons or causes.

Optimism is closely linked to longer, healthier, and more productive lives. Major research studies in the USA, Europe, and Japan show that optimism is strongly related to protection from cardiovascular disease, even when traditional risk factors such as obesity, smoking, alcohol consumption, and hypertension are controlled for. Likely explanations include the way optimists tend to adopt healthier life-styles and have more social support, while genetic factors may also play a part. However, the research is still not clear on the relative roles played by each. Some people seem to be born with the gift of realistic optimism, but extensive research studies have shown that *optimism (like helplessness) can be learned.* [4]

There is, of course, the risk that some people experience too much (unrealistic) optimism, and have a highly inflated sense of self-esteem. Related to this, Carol Dweck at Stanford University has researched what she calls the fixed mindset.[5] Believing that one's qualities are carved in stone—*the fixed mindset*—creates an urgency to prove oneself over and over. There is one consuming goal—look smart, don't look dumb. Every situation is evaluated: Will I succeed or fail? Will I look smart or dumb? Will I be accepted or rejected? Will I feel like a winner or a loser? The drawbacks to this mindset are (i) an anxiety to be seen as successful, (ii) an extreme discomfort with feedback, and (iii) a reluctance to experiment and take risks, which slows down learning from experience. By contrast, the growth mindset is based on the belief that one's basic qualities can be culti-vated through individual effort—everyone can change and grow through application and experience. The fixed mindset is a kind of rigid false optimism. The growth mindset is a source of individual resilience.

Martin Seligman has summarized research on optimism, which shows that:

- Optimists experience less distress than pessimists when dealing with difficulties in their lives.
- They tend to adapt better to negative events in their lives.
- Optimism is related to superior problem-solving, coping, humour, making plans, constructive re-framing, and accepting reality (when nothing can be done).
- Optimists learn from setbacks, and do not blame themselves as much.
- Optimists are not in denial, they face reality, and discover prob-lems quicker than pessimists.
- They do not give up as quickly.
- They are more likely to engage in healthy living, and have better health.
- They are more productive at work.

Seligman argues that the brain registers the experience of optimism and, through chemical and neural pathways, affects cellular functioning throughout the body, including the cardiac, immune, and other systems.

Because optimism is correlated with motivation and taking action, optimistic people are more likely to want to be healthy and to believe they can be healthy. This makes it more likely that they will follow healthy regimens and take medical advice on board. Optimists experience fewer noxious events in their lives than pessimists, including fewer threats to their health, because their sense of control assures them that they can make a difference in what happens. Optimists enjoy greater social support than pessimists, and evidence shows that even mild social interaction is a buffer against both physical and mental illness.

Persistent and unrelenting pessimism can be as unhelpful as naive and unrealistic optimism. Occasionally, we suffer setbacks, disappointments, or crises in our lives and it is natural to feel depressed and anxious. *The key difference between optimists and pessimists is that optimists tend to recover more quickly and start taking action, making plans, renewing goals etc.* Martin Seligman's research showed that pessimists get depressed much more quickly than optimists do, and they underachieve in the classroom, in sports, in their jobs, and in their relationships.

Some people already know whether they are inclined to be optimistic or pessimistic most of the time. Others can go online and complete a short questionnaire to assess their level of dispositional optimism.[6]

Disputing one's pessimistic assumptions is a well-researched method for increasing optimism, developed at the well-evaluated Penn Resilience Program for reducing pessimism and depression in schoolchildren. The exercise takes practice to do well. These are the key steps:

1. Think of a recent setback or disappointment. It can be anything like the following:
   - You did not get a promotion you really wanted.
   - You received an unexpectedly bad performance rating.
   - Your well-prepared proposal, on which a lot was riding, was rejected.
   - A mistake you made at work was openly criticized by your manager.

- Something has been worrying you at work.
- A close relationship at work went sour.

2. What was your reaction? What did you think? How did you feel? How did you apportion blame? Think of any negative thoughts or beliefs about yourself or your situation (problems or setbacks). Write them down.

Disputing pessimistic assumptions:

Describe the disappointment or event as specifically as possible.

Describe how it made you feel about yourself and your role in the event.

Now answer the following questions with vigor and energy to dispute the beliefs you automatically have about yourself. Do the exercise for each belief about yourself you listed above. The idea is to become skilled at generating alternative ways of thinking.

What is the actual evidence for this belief about you? Be as specific as you can.

- What are alternative ways of viewing it? (Especially those that are changeable, specific to circumstances, and not personal to you).
- What is the worst-case scenario? How bad is it really?
- What are the consequences of holding onto this negative belief about you?
- How do you feel about it now?

Here is an example:

Setback: Threatened redundancy.

Emotional response: This kind of thing always happens to me. I always make a mess of things at work.

Evidence: Remember the times when such threats came to nothing. What is the actual evidence that you caused this to happen? What is the actual evidence that you always make a mess of things? Think of your successes and when things were going well? What is different now?

Alternative viewpoints: It might not happen. What action can you take to make it less likely? If it did happen, how serious a problem is it? Can it be seen as an opportunity? What good might come of it? What good has come of unplanned changes in the past? Taking a longer-term view of your life, how can you derive gains rather than losses?

Consequences of holding on to the pessimistic thoughts: Become passive and negative. Increase the likelihood that I will come out of this badly. Might miss out on opportunities. Feel frustrated. Could harm my health.

Feel now (consequences of changing thinking): Less helpless, more ready to take charge and manage this.

---

3. Challenge (dispute) and change your negative beliefs. As we described in Chapter 1, it is your *B*eliefs (B) about an adversity or a setback, and not the *A*dversity (A) itself that triggers the *C*onsequent (C) emotion or feelings. If you have persistent feelings of self-blame, and see your problems as permanent and pervasive, a good way to start climbing out of a dangerous downward spiral is to start disputing self-beliefs. Change the beliefs, and the consequent negative emotions begin to give way to optimism, energy, and hope.

2. Re-framing problems

A version of the cognitive technique can be applied to "re-frame" problems. This is a useful skill to learn so that one begins to see the possibilities in situations that had previously been seen only as problems. In the left-hand column below are examples of problems, and in the right-hand column examples of how they can be re-framed into more creative options and opportunities. It is important to note that each person needs to work out a new perspective that is realistic, believable, and helpful for them. Managers and

Problem	How could it be re-framed?
A problem: My company is being taken over	What opportunities might be there? Could I change roles? How can I make my experience more saleable?
A threat: I might lose my job	What challenges does this present that I could rise to? What can I learn from this? What should I do differently? How can I show my true strengths?
A duty: I hate speaking in public	In what respects is it a privilege? What are potential benefits to me? How can I maximize them?
A chore: I hate filling in these forms	How could I get pleasure or satisfaction out of it? Could I streamline or systematize the process? Could I learn to like it? Could I set myself challenges to meet?
A job: I hate my work	How could I turn it into a sense of vocation? How can I find ways to value and appreciate more what I have to do? What are the good things about it that I could do more of?
A mistake you made	What can I learn from this? What led up to it? How can I avoid repeating it? (See learning from mistakes in the next chapter.)

others can suggest more positive perspectives, but these will not make any difference unless they are relevant and meaningful to the person concerned.

As you read through these examples, it will become very clear that each person has to dispute their own assumptions and find alternative, positive thoughts that they find realistic, meaningful, and believable. For example, the idea of turning a hated job into a sense of vocation may trigger an insightful solution for one person, while others see it as ridiculous and unhelpful. It can be very hard work to find the alternative thoughts that work for you, but it is well worth the effort as the results can be life-changing.

The following format for *perspective taking* is a useful tool for seeing problems or challenges in a new light. It can be used in conjunction with *merit-finding* described below. The basic steps are:

Think of a current problem, setback, or disappointment. Describe the problem as specifically as possible. Describe in a few words how you feel about it.

- On a scale of 1 to 100 rate the problem based on how you feel about it now, where 100 is very bad and 1 is not really a problem at all.
- Now write down some of the worst things you could ever imagine happening to you or in anyone's life. These are 90 to 100 on your scale. Think of terminal cancer, the loss of a child or a loved one, complete destruction by fire of your home.
- How do you feel about your problem now? What number would you give your problem now?
- What can you now do to begin addressing it one step at a time?

3. *Becoming a merit-finder*

Becoming a merit-finder helps develop a positive attitude. As Henry David Thoreau put it, "The fault finder will find faults even in Paradise." According to research studies people who tend to look for the good in people and events tend to have greater well-being, better health, and live longer—all contributors to individual resilience.[8]

Try the following exercise to help you understand the merit-finder approach. Briefly describe a problem or situation you are having a hard time with. Now try and find at least five good or potentially good things about the situation. Be as creative and imaginative as you can.

> *Problem*: My department is being merged with another and I will lose status.
>
> *Potential merits*: It could broaden my experience; I will get closer to new people; I can show how adaptable I am as a manager; I will potentially have access to more senior people; it will be an opportunity to show my loyalty; I can show my appreciation of the wider context; I can show that I manage change positively.

Develop the habit of seeking the potential good in any situation or problem you are dealing with. Keep going for at least two to three weeks. Enlist the help of your friends. Ask them for ideas, offer your own ideas, keep a diary, and you will see your ability to find merit growing with experience. Notice the effect of merit-finding on how you feel.

4. *Avoiding your thinking traps*

Over the years, researchers have investigated the way our thinking habits can trap us into negative and unhelpful thoughts.[9] We also know that the way we think about things has a strong influence over our emotions. Consider the Thinking Traps described below. The process works by describing in some detail a problem and then asking the following questions:

1. *All or none thinking.* Are you seeing the problem in black and white terms? (Example: Nothing good can come out of this takeover.)
2. Are you looking at it in a *blinkered* or too narrow a way, for example, focusing on only the negative comments made by your manager and ignoring other important aspects? (Example: This is just more work for us.)
3. Are you *jumping to conclusions*, assuming you know? (Example: We will all be laid off.) Do you have all the facts? Do you have any facts?
4. Are you *exaggerating or minimizing* the real picture? (Example: It's a disaster or It doesn't really matter.) How does it compare? Have you checked? Are you keeping things in perspective, taking a balanced view?

5. Are your *emotions/fears holding sway* over your reasoning? Are you reacting emotionally (Example: I feel anxious, so I must have done something wrong)? What are the facts? Is the language you are using mostly emotional rather than factual?
6. Are you *boxing yourself into a corner*, where you see only one option? (Example: If they won't talk to me then I am certainly not going to talk to them.)
7. Are you labeling people or things in more *extreme* terms than they deserve, or stereotyping them (Example: I'm a disaster... They're lazy)?
8. Are you *blaming yourself* for things outside your control? (Example: I should have known better than to join this company!)

Recognizing these traps is the first step to avoiding them. Over time it is possible to build up an armory of helpful alternative thoughts that circumvent these thinking traps, and stay on a more positive and realistic track.

INCREASING POSITIVE EMOTIONS: THE SECOND BROAD APPROACH TO RESILIENCE-BUILDING

Although emotions are a core element of the cognitive approach to resilience described above, in this context they are referred to mainly as the outcome of thoughts and beliefs, and the whole emphasis of the approach is on reducing negative emotions by getting rid of unhelpful, inaccurate negative beliefs and assumptions. More recent developments highlight the benefit of a complementary approach that focuses directly on positive emotions, and we saw in Chapter 1 that a powerful way to build individual resilience is to increase the amount of positive emotion in one's life. In the following discussion, we recap briefly and expand on the shift to Positive Psychology that we have described in previous chapters, and then explore in more detail its practical implications for resilience-building.

To begin with, we take another look at the more familiar notion of "negative emotions" such as anger, fear, anxiety, and sadness—this time from an evolutionary or biological perspective. Most people are aware that *anger* or *fear* creates a fight or flight response in our bodies, readying us for quick action that may help us survive attack or potential danger. This is what happens when the body goes into such a state of arousal:

- Blood sugar becomes elevated; cortisol and adrenaline enter the blood stream.
- Heart rate speeds up to pump blood to the muscles for instant fighting or a short burst of running.
- Red blood cells become "sticky" to increase clotting if wounded.
- The pupils in the eyes widen, you breathe harder and faster, and you perspire.
- Immune-system functions decrease and digestion slows down.

The reflex system that controls the response to negative emotions is in the genes and is universal.

Even though these emotions help you to deal with a crisis, you are not always at your best when you feel them. Bill Ury, the author of *Getting to Yes*, once said: "when you are angry you will make the best speech you will ever regret." We also know from experience and many research studies that anger distorts decision-making and makes people defensive and uncooperative.

"Negative emotions" put you in a body state that readies you for quick action without having to think. The trouble with these emotions is their damaging effects if they persist too long. If arousal from stress or worry continues unabated for weeks and months, diseases of adaptation develop. This can include high blood pressure, heart attacks, strokes, and various forms of cancer. Anxiety or fear in the face of real threat, or the occasional anxiety about a real or threatened loss, are normal and adaptive. Such emotions can even make us stronger, but on the whole we much prefer to experience positive emotions.

Until quite recently, there had been twenty times as much published scientific research into negative emotions such as anger and anxiety as published research into positive emotions such as love, gratitude, and hope.[10] This was understandable given the need to understand and help people suffering from depression and other psychological problems such as anxiety and personality disorders. However, this imbalance in research has resulted in a lop-sided understanding of human emotion. Psychology as a science was very effective in describing, diagnosing, and treating depression and anxiety disorders, but had little to say on what contributes to and builds qualities such as resilience, hope, and happiness. This, unfortunately, left the almost insatiable human demand for guidance on how to be happy, fulfilled, or satisfied with life wide open to the self-help industry with a panoply of books, CDs, workshops, and mobile apps to fill the gap. Not all such advice is wrong or misleading, but there is often a lack of scientific evidence to support or explain the advice that is being given.

The rise of Positive Psychology, signaled by Martin Seligman at his Presidential Address to the American Psychological Association in 1998, has led to a dramatically increased research focus on what makes people flourish, the qualities that help people be happy, and the kinds of institutions (communities, work-places) that enable people to be at their best. Over the past fifteen years, positive emotions and the role they play in personal well-being and effectiveness have been extensively and scientifically researched by, among others, Barbara Fredrickson and her colleagues at the University of North Carolina, Chapel Hill in the United States.[11] There is even a branch of Positive Psychology that focuses primarily on the workplace, and this is called Positive Organizational Scholarship.[12]

Positive human emotions that have been subjected to this new, intensive research interest in the past ten to fifteen years include *joy, gratitude, serenity, interest, hope, pride, humor, inspiration, awe, love, forgiveness*, and *compassion*. We have known for many years that negative emotions, which humans share with many other species, evolved because they had survival value. It was understood that negative emotions in general alerted people to danger, and that quick, unthinking actions were required to reach a safe state. Each negative emotion was associated with a specific action-tendency. It has long been known that fear generates a fight, flight, freeze action pattern, and that anger generates a desire for attack or revenge, and nausea leads to avoidance.

It was only in the past decade, however, that we began to understand that positive emotions also evolved because they had survival value—especially when early hominids began to live and hunt in small groups where social cohesiveness and collaboration contributed to survival of the group. This became even more significant when early humans transitioned from hunting and gathering into settled communities based on herding and agriculture which came into existence only about 10,000 years ago.[13] In short, negative emotions are associated with alerting the sympathetic nervous system that puts the individual into a high state of arousal, while positive emotions are associated with activity in the calming parasympathetic nervous system that makes one receptive to new experiences.

Barbara Fredrickson and her researchers have taken the theory one step further. They argue that positive emotions not only serve to tell people they are safe and help make them effective in the present, but also build capability and make people stronger to deal with future adversities and setbacks. This is the *Strengthen and Build Theory*, which is rapidly gaining support from other fields of inquiry such as neuroscience and biology as well as from extensive psychological research. Here is a list of some of the beneficial effects of experiencing positive emotion, based on experimental studies where volunteers were deliberately led to experience positive or negative emotions.[14]

Beneficial effects of increasing levels of positive emotion are listed below:

- It becomes easier to connect ideas, to be creative.
- It becomes easier to connect with others.
- Decision-making improves.
- Open-mindedness and curiosity increases.
- Peripheral vision improves.
- Physical health improves.
- Helping-behavior (altruism) is increased.
- An increased sense of "we" rather than "me" is experienced.
- Perceptions of "them and us" are reduced.
- There is greater willingness to accommodate ambiguity or uncertainty.
- Handling of complexity is improved.
- Emotional agility is stimulated.

Overall, positive emotions help build psychological strengths, good mental habits, social connections, and physical health, and contribute significantly to resilience. They are not a luxury or a "nice to have," but are essential ingredients to people's effectiveness at work and their lives as a whole.

Clearly you cannot experience positive emotions all the time. Those people who do are often felt to be out of touch with reality and can be experienced by others as intensely annoying. There are times when you must feel angry, worried, or disappointed but if you spend too much time experiencing negative emotion, or take too long to bounce back, there is a risk that you undermine your own effectiveness. It is well known that people who spend extensive periods feeling stressed or worried find that their personal efficacy and health is seriously weakened. Barbara Fredrickson's research shows that there is a critical ratio of positive to negative emotions in our lives. Below that point negative emotions are weakening us. Above that point our positive emotions are strengthening us.

If your ratio for the past 24 hours is below 3 positive emotions to 1 negative emotion (e.g. a ratio of 2 to 1), you probably had a "not so good" day. If your ratio was well above 3 to 1, you probably had a good, or even a great day. Your ratio for one day however is not really a concern. Just as the saying goes, one swallow does not make a summer. What is of concern is how often your ratio for any 24-hour period is well below 3 to 1. If your averaged ratio for 14 days is below 3 to 1, you may be experiencing and living with sustained negative emotions that could be undermining your resilience and general health, and this will have direct implications for your effectiveness at work. By contrast, a sustained ratio above 3 to 1 over several weeks suggests that you have the emotional strength to deal with stresses at work and in your life as a whole. In effect, you are flourishing rather than floundering, despite the pressures, disappointment, and setbacks that are part of everyday life.

You can go online to measure your own positivity ratio.[15] The Positivity Self Test can be completed on a regular basis to monitor progress, say every three to six months. The positivity ratio does not have the reliability and accuracy of a conventional thermometer as an indicator of ill-health, or of health for that matter. It is still in development as a research tool, but it is accurate enough to give individual users an indication of their emotional strength in the face of adversity, and it can also be used to set targets for personal improvement and to evaluate change over time.

In summary, positive emotions have four powerful effects:

- They help undo the harmful effects of stress.
- They help you return to normal more quickly after feeling stressed.

- They help buffer you from the harmful or negative effects of stress.
- They strengthen you to cope with life's challenges and setbacks in the future.

Having looked at the two *broad approaches* for developing resilience, we turn in the next chapter to a discussion of how to boost each of the four main components of resilience.

CHAPTER 5

WHAT INDIVIDUALS CAN DO: STRENGTHENING THE FOUR PERSONAL RESILIENCE RESOURCES

The relevance of the two broad approaches (the cognitive approach and increasing positive emotions) that we described in the previous chapter will be briefly highlighted at appropriate points during the following discussion on developing the four components of resilience (the personal resilience resources), but we will not repeat the detailed accounts already provided. It should also be pointed out that, as implied by the overlapping circles in Figure 5.1, the specific techniques we discuss below may apply to more than one of the four components.

As in Chapter 4, we suggest that you work through the material provided here with your own resilience in mind, as this will strengthen your understanding of the principles and techniques and help you to select the most useful for your purpose.

CONFIDENCE

Core techniques: (i) apply the cognitive approach—challenge any negative assumptions about your own abilities, "re-frame," face your fears, use reflection; (ii) identify and use your natural strengths; (iii) get into "flow"—stretch yourself by taking on challenges.

Applying the cognitive approach

This approach is particularly well suited to increasing resilience by improving self-confidence/self-belief. Refer to the detailed account

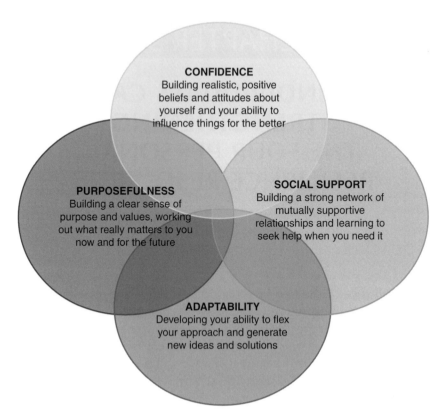

FIGURE 5.1 **Building resilience: the four personal resilience resources**

in Chapter 4, and also to the section on optimism and explanatory style in Chapter 1.

Using reflection to boost resilience

A habit of reflecting on the present and recent past can have a powerful effect on how we see and cope with the present and the future. Questions to ask yourself routinely include:

- What went well at work today? This week?
- What did I enjoy?
- When did I feel at my best?
- What did not go so well, why?
- How can I avoid it, change it, think about it differently?

- What can I do to get more positives into my day/week, and fewer negatives?

Identifying and using natural strengths to boost resilience

Getting in touch with and using natural strengths is a significant contributor to resilience. *Spotting Strengths*[1] is a helpful exercise that helps identify natural strengths:

- What did you enjoy doing as a child?
- What activities energize you?
- When do you feel most authentic as a person?
- What comes easily to you?
- What do you pay most attention to?
- What do you learn easily and rapidly?
- What motivates you?
- Where do you speak with a genuine voice?
- What words do you tend to use when you are energized and engaged?
- What do you do spontaneously without effort?

A "strength" in this context is something you do well as a human being that feels as though it comes naturally; it requires no effort as you feel energized not drained. You relish doing it. This kind of "natural strength" is different from skills that require repetition and practice to achieve, such as learning to drive a car. People are often at their best when they are using their strengths. They feel authentic and energised. Knowing and using strengths, especially in different ways or contexts, has been shown to reduce stress and boost resilience. It is common to put too much focus on remedying weaknesses, which can be hard work and often unfulfilling. There are real benefits to finding and going with your natural strengths. Energy is a hallmark feature of such strengths, and is fundamental to identifying them.

Donald Clifton worked with the Gallup Organization, along with Marcus Buckingham, and is one of the pioneers of the "strengths-based approach" to people management.[2] He argued that discovering and harnessing one's natural talents provides the greatest opportunities for success. He recommended everyone should work with the qualities they have rather than the ones they wish they had.

Christopher Peterson and Martin Seligman have identified the criteria for signature strengths. These include *a sense of ownership and authenticity* ("this is the real me"), *a feeling of excitement while displaying it*, particularly at first, *a rapid learning curve, a sense of yearning, a feeling of inevitability*, and *invigoration* rather than exhaustion when using the strength.[3] Personal strengths of this kind can be assessed online in three different ways, each with different benefits to the individual.

1. *VIA Inventory of Strengths (VIA-IS), formerly referred to as Values in Action*

This survey rank-orders the character strengths from 1 to 24 (listed in the box that follows) and helps individuals identify their top character strengths, also referred to as signature strengths. This list represents the outcome of a major study carried out by Christopher Peterson (University of Michigan) and Martin Seligman (University of Pennsylvania) to find the values that all societies, religious traditions, and cultures through-out the world now and in the past have upheld and pursued for their own sake. The six virtues are achieved or expressed by means of the human strengths that are associated with each one.

Wisdom and Knowledge 1. Creativity 2. Curiosity 3. Judgement 4. Love of learning 5. Perspective

Courage 1. Bravery 2. Perseverance 3. Honesty 4. Zest

Humanity 1. Love 2. Kindness 3. Social intelligence

Justice 1. Teamwork 2. Fairness 3. Leadership

Temperance 1. Forgiveness 2. Humility 3. Prudence 4. Self-Regulation

Transcendence 1. Appreciation of beauty and excellence 2. Gratitude 3. Hope 4. Humor 5. Spirituality

---

Signature strengths help define the individual as a person. Being aware of them helps find paths and activities that enable one to feel authentic, energized and true to oneself. A great deal of research has been carried out using the VIA Strengths.[4]

Making the use of these strengths a part of longer term life and career goals, increases the likelihoood that one will succeed in life. Finding and using "signature strengths" in different contexts has a strong link to well-being, and has been shown to reduce the effects of anxiety and stress, thus contributing indirectly to individual resilience. Signature strengths can be assessed online.[5]

The VIA Signature Strengths approach is geared to the context of general personal development and resilience-building. When it comes to developing strengths to enhance your overall effectiveness and success at work, it is important to identify and make the most of your signature strengths, while also developing a wider range of skills and capabilities to ensure you are able to perform your role with confidence and competence.

2. Realise2

The second approach to strengths assessment is Realise2.[6] This instrument is published by the Centre for Applied Positive Psychology in the UK, and is based on 60 separate strengths divided into five families:

- Being, e.g. Strengths of Authenticity, Mission, Legacy
- Communicating, e.g. Strengths of Listener, Feedback, Humor
- Motivating, e.g. Strengths of Bounce-back, Growth, Change Agent
- Relating, e.g. Strengths of Compassion, Relationship Deepener, Connector
- Thinking, e.g. Strengths of Order, Adherence, Creativity, Resolver

Realise2 can be very powerful for personal development planning, and in coaching, where the focus is on more specific strengths than the 24 character strengths in the VIA assessment. Whereas VIA is primarily about character strengths, Realise2 strengths overlap with personality characteristics and other learned abilitiies. Realise2 has a powerful feature that divides strengths into four broad categories:

1. *Realized Strengths*—these are performed well, and they are energizing but there is a need to avoid the danger of over-relying on them, or taking them to extremes, i.e. their use should be marshalled.

2. *Unrealized Strengths*—these are performed well, they are energizing, and opportunities should be found to maximize their use.
3. *Learned Behaviors*—these are performed well but this may be de-energizing, and their use should be moderated.
4. *Weaknesses*—these are performed poorly, and unless critical should be minimzed or balanced out with other strengths.

Realise2 generates individual and team development reports which can be very helpful for balancing development planning between building on strengths, especially the unrealized ones, and efforts to recognize and deal with weaknesses that may have critical effects on job performance. Realise2 is supported by *The Strengths Book*[7] which offers many ideas for developing each of the 60 strengths. A small charge is made for the online assessment, and a personal development report can be produced.

3. StrengthsFinder

The third approach is StrengthsFinder, published and based on research by the Gallup Organization. In this case the strengths are more work-related, and they number 34 in all. Access to the online assessment comes with purchase of books published by Gallup[8] or through direct online purchase. There is an option to have development ideas linked to identified strengths. This can be helpful in the absence of any other guidance on personal development in the workplace.[9]

Once strengths have been identified using one of these three tools, it is helpful to consider these questions:

- What did you learn about yourself from identifying your strengths?
- Which strengths have you developed; which do you use in your work?
- Are there strengths you are not using at work which are evident in your private life?
- Are there strengths you are not using in your private life which are evident in your work life?
- Are you making optimum use of your strengths to help you perform at your best at work?
- What opportunities are there for you to make more or different use of your strengths at work?

- What opportunities are there for you to make more or different use of your strengths in other parts of your life?
- What are the shadow sides of your strengths (e.g. the risks of over-using certain strengths), and how can you minimize these?

Getting into FLOW to help build resilience

In this section, we introduce a new angle by looking at what happens when strengths and skills are put to the test by challenges or tasks that stretch but do not overwhelm.

This exercise helps the individual identify challenges that stretch but do not overwhelm:

Make a list of skilled activities you enjoy at work so much that you sometimes lose a sense of time, a sense of yourself and come out of it invigorated.

Make a list of skilled activities you enjoy in the rest of your life, so much that you sometimes lose a sense of time and yourself, and come out of it invigorated.

Now make a list of skilled activities you used to love doing when you were younger (and were good at) that you no longer do or have too little time to do these days.

The things you list are likely to be sources of FLOW, which is a state of total absorption that comes about when skills and challenge are optimally balanced. It is sometimes defined as the experience of working at full capacity. Flow is pleasurable in its own right, but when Flow is linked to higher goals and contributing to others this can be deeply satisfying. Experiencing this can make you feel elevated (a warm feeling, opening up, lighter). Flow is particularly invigorating and satisfying when applied to a challenge that is neither too easy nor too difficult. Flow has been extensively researched over many years by Mihaly Csikszentmihalyi now at Claremont Graduate University in California.[10]

The following are conditions and signs of FLOW:

- The task is challenging and requires skill.
- You concentrate.

- There are clear goals.
- You get immediate feedback.
- You have deep effortless involvement.
- There is a sense of control.
- Your sense of self vanishes.
- Time stops.

There is good evidence demonstrating that Flow contributes to higher performance and satisfaction, and to increased motivation, creativity, self-esteem and happiness. The things you used to do when you were younger, and had more freedom, were probably things that created Flow—whether these activities involved rock climbing, playing sports, music, acting, dominoes or painting etc. Studying Flow indicates that these activities are not luxuries in life but rather essentials that contribute significantly to well-being and resilience. Activities that create Flow also help de-stress you, and buffer you against the harmful effects of negative emotions such as stress and anxiety. You need to have Flow producing activities in all areas of life, work as well as non-work.

Getting into Flow is fundamental to well-being, performance and satisfaction. It may help to recognise that there is more than just one kind of intelligence that one can tap into. Howard Gardner at Harvard University has identified distinct intelligences.[11] Each person is likely to achieve Flow in one or more of the following areas, where he or she feels at their best:

- skill with words;
- skill with numbers;
- spatial thinking/reasoning;
- body co-ordination (kinaesthetic);
- musical ability;
- interpersonal ability;
- intrapersonal ability;
- naturalistic/outdoors.

ASSESSING AND CHANGING YOUR TIME PERSPECTIVES

Research carried out by Stanford psychologist Phillip Zimbardo has identified five broad time perspectives which at different points of our lives exist side by side to varying degrees.[12] These individual attitudes toward time are learned through personal experience as well as cultural influences. Zimbardo showed that time is one of the most powerful influences on our thoughts, feelings, and actions, yet we are usually totally unaware of the effect of time in our lives. Each time perspective is associated with advantages and costs when over-used.

1. The past-negative perspective focuses on negative personal experiences that still have the power to upset you. This can lead to feelings of bitterness and regret.
2. The past-positive perspective takes a nostalgic view of the past. Relationships and memories are likely to be positive but the downside is that if taken to extremes the person becomes risk averse and inclined to play safe.
3. The present-hedonistic perspective is dominated by pleasure-seeking impulses, and this can reduce the discipline needed to forego present pleasures in the interests of future gain. One may be popular but can be associated with unhealthy lifestyle and risk-taking.
4. The present-fatalistic perspective is associated with enjoying the present but feel trapped in it, and a feeling of powerlessness in regards to the future.
5. The future-focused perspective is associated with ambition, goal setting, and "to do" lists. There can sometimes be a sense of urgency that can be a source of stress for yourself and those around you. Too much focus on the future can come at the cost of close relationships and time to relax and recuperate.

In general, the ideal time perspective, to avoid stress and maximize life satisfaction, is low past-negative, high past-positive, low present-fatalism, and moderately high (but not very high) on both present-hedonism, and future-focused. The Zimbardo Time Perspective Inventory can be taken online at http://www.thetimeparadox.com/research/

SOCIAL SUPPORT

Core techniques: (i) develop your emotional intelligence; (ii) maintain engagement in social activity; (iii) expand and take care of your relationships; (iv) express gratitude.

Developing emotional intelligence

See Chapter 1 for an overview of emotional (or "hot") intelligence—incorporating the competencies of self-awareness, self-management, social awareness, and social skills—and its relevance to resilience-building. Exercising emotional intelligence is essential to the development and maintenance of strong, supportive relationships, and as indicated by the use of the term "competency," the elements of emotional intelligence can be developed.

Engaging in social activity and building relationships

Social support and good relationships help build and sustain personal resilience. Extensive research studies have shown that happy people tend to their relationships with the same care a gardener might to his or her plants. It has been argued that working briefly on personal relationships every day, will do more for individual health and longevity than working out at a health club—and there is no doubt that physical activity above a critical threshold has a powerful positive impact on well-being and resilience as we shall see later in this chapter.

Over millions of years, the human brain has evolved to be social, and to live and function in groups. It is in a very real sense a "social brain." It needs interaction with others to learn the skills for surviving and thriving. There was clearly evolutionary benefit in evolving genes that encouraged social living, cooperation and collaboration. Individual resilience is partly dependent on our entire social network. There is growing research evidence to show that actively connecting to others in positive and compassionate ways increases individual resilience.[13] Benefits include:

- mutual appreciation and togetherness;
- recharging our batteries and a sense of vitality;
- physiological changes associated with well-being.

A review of the published research concluded that good relationships with others may be the single most important source of life satisfaction and emotional well-being across people of all ages and cultures.[14] The following are some of the most important findings.

Relationships based on trust, intimacy and affection have a particularly strong association with health and well-being. Strong relationships help to build a feeling of engagement and connectedness with the world. These relationships can play a powerful role in creating a sense of purpose and meaning in life. Someone's degree of social cohesion and relatedness with other people, is one of the most powerful predictors of his or her success during periods of challenge and stress. It is not just our relationships that are important, but also our skills in dealing with others. IQ predicts only 25% of career success; the rest is a combination of our ability to manage energy and stress, our social networks of support, and a belief that one's behaviour really matters.[15]

There are several things you can do to improve social relationships at work—and outside work, as the same skills apply. Four useful things to do are:

1. Map and strengthen your social networks.
2. Improve problematic or strained relationships.
3. Respond actively and constructively to others instead of passively and negatively.
4. Balance Advocacy with Inquiry when seeking to influence others.

Mapping social networks is a good place to start, to see whether there is scope for enlarging them or benefitting more from them. By "mapping different networks," you can assess the social resources available to you, and identify areas where they could be strengthened. This is beneficial, as it is well established that people who are lonely and disconnected from others are more prone to pessimism, ill-health and depression. Having mapped the resources, it is up to you to take the intiative to open up and develop relationships using some of the techniques described below.

The power of networks lies in their exponential potential. If you know three people who each know three other people, you have access to nine people. If each of these people knows three others, the number jumps to 27. Very rapidly, large numbers of people are within reach.

Kevin Bickart at Boston University has shown that a certain area of the brain is larger in people who belong to wider and/or more complex social networks. This area is the amygdala, a structure located in the medial temporal lobes of the brain. The amygdala is involved in emotional learning, and probably evolved to cope with increasingly complex social life as humans evolved.[16]

There are different kinds of network that can be mapped at work:

- "trust network" (Who do, or can, you confide in?);
- "advice network" (Who do you turn to for advice and guidance?);
- "information network" (Who do you turn to for information you need?);
- "socialising network" (Who do you like being with, having fun with?).

Take the following steps to apply this to your own situation. For each network, list the people at work you already have contact with. Think of the actual and potential benefits. Is it a two-way street? Think of people you could add to the network. Think of potential benefits to you and to them. Confiding relationships where we feel confident enough to disclose how we really feel are especially important in our lives. Establish at least one new confiding relationship. Who might this be? How will you do it? Try opening up an existing relationship by small amounts over a period of time.

Practice *improving problematic or strained relationships* by identifying at least two relationships at work that are not as good as they might be. For each of these relationships try making them FAST. Think how to make each relationship better by:

- injecting humor and warmth, and having more *Fun*, enjoying the interaction itself, not just because it leads somewhere;
- showing *Attention* and interest, asking more questions and listening genuinely;
- offering *Support*, even unexpectedly;
- showing *Trust*, acceptance, approval and acceptance.

Very often a relationship can feel strained because you have unwittingly approached it with a negative frame of mind, which tends to produce negative experience for both you and the other/s involved. Taking the initiative to change the emotional tone of the relationship can produce rapid, self-reinforcing changes for the better.

Responding constructively to others builds relationships, even where there is no particular barrier problem to resolve. The work of Shelly Gable[17] at University of California, Santa Barbara shows that when an individual responds actively and constructively (as opposed to passively and destructively) to someone sharing an experience, the relationship is strengthened and becomes more positive. Consider when somebody—a friend, colleague or a relative stranger—tells you about something good that has happened. You can respond in one of four basic ways, only one of which strengthens the relationship. Take the example of a situation where someone tells you that they have just been promoted. The four styles of responding are presented in the table that follows.

Active-constructive	Authentic, enthusiastic support	That's great. Tell me what's involved? When did this happen? How are you feeling? That will make a real difference to so many people.
Passive-constructive	Indifferent support	That's nice. (Nothing more)
Passive-destructive	Ignoring the event	Just wait till I tell you my news.
Active-destructive	Pointing out negative aspects of the event	I hope you know what you are undertaking. I have heard only bad stories.

Responding to the details of what someone has said demonstrates that you are listening, noticing, and are interested. Try and identify the situations and the people with whom you are most likely to adopt the three unhelpful ways of responding. For example, it may happen when you are tired, pre-occupied, very busy, or with people you dislike. Set yourself the task of responding constructively in situations where you would like to improve your impact on others, or the quality of your relationships with them.

Balancing advocacy with inquiry is the converse of active, constructive responding and is most relevant when you are seeking to influence or persuade others to your point of view. The difference lies in getting the balance right between *Advocating* (arguing for what you want) and *Inquiring* (understanding what others want).

Advocacy involves presenting your thoughts and ideas, telling people what you want, using your skills, knowledge and experience to tell or sell your ideas, and focusing on your agenda and needs. By contrast, *Inquiry* involves seeking others' thoughts and ideas, asking people what they want to happen, using others' skills, knowledge, and experience, and focusing on their agenda. Getting the balance between Advocacy and Inquiry right is a skill that strengthens relationships and avoids sinking into antagonisms and conflict.

Inquiry mode behaviors include:

- Ask, listen, and explain; avoid just telling and selling.
- Try to react not with a judgment, but with an inquiry.
- Avoid giving your views so strongly that you discourage debate.
- Stress the wider good, not just your needs.
- Show that you understand where the other person is coming from; what are the buttons to press?
- Stress realistic costs/risks as well as benefits.
- Ensure the purpose or objective is clear to all.

Getting the balance right between Advocacy and Inquiry builds trust and openness. People feel respected and are less likely to withhold their true views by staying silent.

Expressing gratitude

"Expressing gratitude" has been proven to create deep and persistent feelings, which reduce the effects of stress and feelings of depression and boost personal resilience.[18] Consider how often you show appreciation, as a manager or as a work colleague, for what others do, or for a job well done. Are your thanks offered in a perfunctory way, with little effort expended, or are they thoughtfully and personally expressed? It is very easy to take others for granted especially when you feel under pressure yourself, and to forget to show empathy and appreciation.

Routinely expressing appreciation and gratitude, on a daily basis, to the people with whom you come into contact, can help boost resilience. Gratitude has a special quality in common with compassion, love and forgiveness. All stand out from other positive emotions in that they benefit the giver and the receiver equally. Exercises in, and the practice of, gratitude formed an important part of the US Army Master Resilience Training, which we describe in Chapter 6.

Small acts of kindness boost the giver's well-being as well as that of others. Researchers found that doing an act of kindness produces the single most reliable, momentary increase in well-being of the many interventions tested. Offers to help and support others, even when under presssure, can deepen human relationships in a way that is intrinsically satisfying, and indirectly contributes to individual resilience.

ADAPTABILITY

Core techniques: (i) develop a range of coping strategies; (ii) learn from your mistakes and take risks; (iii) exercise your imagination; (iv) stretch yourself, learn new skills; (v) look after your physical condition.

Developing a range of coping strategies

To build resilience it is important to develop a range of coping strategies, rather than relying too heavily on one or two—no matter how well these may seem to be working. For example, people who are naturally keen on order and structure often rely on planning and organization as their main coping strategy. This is effective in many situations, but may let them down in times of rapid change, or when they are dependent on others to provide information or make decisions. To expand your ways of coping, the first step is to identify what pressures you are particularly susceptible to, and the strategies you typically use to manage them. The material we have provided in this and other chapters can be drawn on to work out your tried-and-tested coping techniques, and to select others you could try to use more frequently or effectively.

Keeping a journal: in this context, we would like to mention the specific technique of keeping a journal. This is an effective method for reducing anxiety and managing stress, which also has the advantage of enabling you to reflect on what causes you stress, how you typically respond, and what makes you feel better.

In 1997, Jamie Pennebaker, of the University of Texas, reported his research on the benefits of keeping a journal, as a way of dealing with stresses and problems. He found that the regular practice of keeping a journal reduced anxiety, and resulted in a 50% drop in visits to a doctor. The immune system and overall health of those who kept a journal improved, as did their general emotional well-being. They also became more social, which is another key booster for individual resilience.

It is now known that routinely keeping a journal can raise well-being and resilience for several months afterwards. In some cases it can help alleviate feelings of depression (especially when done in conjunction with regular physical exercise).

Tips for applying this technique

Keeping a record at the end of most days of *Three Good Things* in the day, is a proven tool for improving resilience and well-being. Alternatively, this can be thought of as a *WWW* (what went well) journal, or simply as a record of three things you are grateful for each day. If you try this technique, it helps to be as specific as possible, to reflect on your own role in each event, and to try and capture your feelings. Your record can include anything that occurs to you, whether simple or profound, concerning family, friends, work, the outdoors, art or beauty etc. The power of the exercise may increase when done with partners, friends or work colleagues. Try and keep the journal going for at least 21 days. It can be a good idea to buy a small note-book for the purpose, or you could use an app that is available for smartphones.[19] The power of keeping a journal lies in doing it on a regular basis but it is not essential to do it all the time.

Some fami,es routinely gather at the end of the day to express gratitude and appreciation, which can strengthen bonding. Many will recognise this as the old adage, "Count Your Blessings." There is now scientific evidence to prove that this long established practice actually makes a difference.[20]

A version of the journal technique that is particularly well suited to increasing *Adaptability* by *expanding your coping strategies* involves keeping a daily record of how you are feeling as you deal with a difficulty or a challenge in your life, such as a lack of clarity about your role, or a period of sustained pressure at work. This is useful even if the pressure you are experiencing is not particularly severe. Describe as accurately as you can what you experience each day. Use the cognitive technique explained in Chapter 4 to reflect on, challenge and re-frame your thoughts and feelings. In addition, reflect on the coping strategies you have used to cope with or recover from the situation—are you using a number of different approaches, or are you relying too heavily on one or two?

Another variation of the journal technique that is directly relevant to *Adaptability*, involves writing about your challenges and difficulties using language that is deliberately more positive (although ideally grounded in realism) than that which first comes to mind. Evidence shows that this actually increases your adaptability in coping with diverse challenges and stresses. The approach is akin to a technique used by the world's most effective and powerful behaviour change program, Alcoholics Anonymous (AA). The AA programs use a technique called "Fake It Until You Can Make It." There is now evidence from neuroscience that the underlying mechanism here is the re-wiring of neural pathways in the brain that help create new habits.

Learning from your mistakes and taking risks

Adaptability can also be improved by learning to face your fears, and increasing your willingness to take risks. This involves recognising that failure and setbacks are not always bad for you. No-one succeeds, or can expect to succeed, all the time. Some of the most powerful lessons in life and at work come from making mistakes or taking risks that do not work out, and it is worth noting that many entrepreneurs have several business failures before they hit the jackpot. Scientific evidence reveals the following benefits that can be derived from failure.[21]

Learning from failure improves Adaptability by:

- promoting reflection on what you are doing and how you could do it better;
- stimulating change by uncovering new problem-solving approaches;
- providing feedback on what went wrong;
- encouraging the flexibility to think beyond your current ways of doing things;
- improving your frustration tolerance for dealing with situations that that fail to turn out the way you expected;
- teaching humility about the limitations of your knowledge and abilities, challenging any tendency to unrealistic self-assurance.

131

Exercising your imagination

As mentioned earlier, if you are by nature a practical, structured and detail-conscious person, these characteristics will have their advantages and disadvantages in helping you to cope with pressure. When it comes to the *Adaptability* component of resilience, a possible tendency to over-rely on planning and organization is not the only risk. A focus on order and practicality will certainly help create a sense of purpose and make it easier for you to plan ahead and take an organized approach to solving problems. However, the danger is that you may close down on a solution without fully exercising your imagination or allowing enough time to generate options and consider alternative possibilities.

Imagination is like a muscle—if you do not exercise it often enough then it is harder to put it into action when you really do need to come up with a different approach or a creative solution. The most important practical tip here is to identify situations where there is scope for considering different solutions—even if you are under no pressure to come up with something new. Then set time aside to make a long list of ideas—the crazier the better—before going through your list to select the best and work them up in more detail. Do this regularly, until you feel confident in your ability to respond flexibly to unexpected situations and challenges.

Stretching yourself, learning new skills

If you never step outside your comfort zone, this can have a surprisingly negative effect on your resilience. Stretching yourself to learn new skills boosts resilience by increasing both confidence and adaptability. These benefits can be achieved even if the challenges you take on and the new skills you learn are unrelated to your work objectives or to the demands of other aspects of your life.

Looking after your physical condition

Being physically fit helps everyone to adapt to difficult conditions and supports resilience in other ways too. Here we look at understanding the physical–biological underpinnings of individual resilience, and the important role played by exercise, sleep and diet. If your physical condition falls below a critical threshold, this can seriously undermine your resilience. Conversely, looking after and "toughening" one's physical condition is a "prescribed" factor for improving resilience.[22]

There is a steadily increasing body of scientific research that shows a strong causal relationship between physical activity, on the one hand, and health, well-being and resilience, on the other. The documented physical benefits of regular physical exercise include fitness and better cardiovascular functioning, a general strengthening of the immune system, stronger muscles and bones (aiding strength and balance), changes to blood lipid profile (reducing the risk of more than a dozen types of cancer), and decreased risk of heart disease, stroke, and diabetes.

If that is not impressive enough, there are distinct psychological benefits of exercise including reduced levels of depression and anxiety, buffering against the toxic effects of stress, enhanced speed and accuracy of work, improved self-concept, improved concentration and reaction times, and a slowing down of physical and mental ageing (positive ageing).

In his book *Brain Rules*, John Medina[23] has summarized some of the dramatic findings about the relationship between physical activity and health, including significant reductions in the risk of Alzheimer's disease, dementia and stroke. When exercise is done in the company of others, there is the added benefit of social bonding. Regular physical exercise is so beneficial that it is now being incorporated into the treatment of people with mild depression, and in some cases it can have longer lasting benefits than medication.[24]

One of the most important underlying mechanisms involves the release, through exercise, of important hormones and neurotransmitters such as serotonin, dopamine, and norepinephrine, which play a key role in feeling good. There is also the benefit derived from increasing the supply of oxygen to the brain. Oxygenating your blood and cells is far more important than hydrating them. One deep breath can calm you. When you are stressed or anxious and your heart is beating faster than 100 bps (beats per second), you cannot hear or pay attention to what is being said to you. Breathing deeply calms you down. Exercise increases blood flow across the body, creating nitric oxide which stimulates creation of new blood vessels, penetrating deep into body tissue. Blood delivers glucose and oxygen to all parts of the body. Glucose releases energy and oxygen transforms toxic waste from cells into transportable carbon dioxide. The more you exercise the more body tissue you can feed and the more toxic waste you can remove all over the body, making you healthier and stronger.

The brain is only 2% of body weight, yet it consumes 20% of the body's energy supply, and in spite of this can only operate 2% of its neurons at any one time as it is limited by glucose supply. Physical exercise helps by making the process of supplying oxygen to the brain less demanding on our bodies, enabling optimum performance. Exercise also stimulates the brain's most powerful growth protein, brain-derived neurotrophic factor also known as BDNF, which acts like a fertiliser to keep existing neurons young and healthy, and to increase their connectivity. Similarly, exercise encourages the formation of new brain cells, especially in the hippocampus, which is closely involved in human cognition.

Checking your physical condition

Regular physical activity of any kind can make you healthier and more energetic, resulting in significant improvements in your physical and psychological functioning. Do you consider yourself reasonably fit and healthy? How do you really know? You can check a variety of measures for yourself:

- Your Fitness Rating is a measure of how well your body can take up oxygen. You can do this with friends and have some fun at the same time.[25]
- Your BMI is a statistical measure of body weight based on height and weight. BMI is only indicative and needs to be combined with other measures such as percentage body fat. It is calculated by dividing your weight in kilos by two times your height in meters.
    - BMI less than 18.5 = under-weight
    - 18.5 to 24.9 = normal weight
    - 25 to 29.9 = over-weight
    - 30 and over = obese
- *Waist hip ratio* (WHR) is your waist measurement divided by your hip measurement. A WHR less than .8 for women and less than 1.0 for men correlates strongly with good general health.
- High blood pressure over sustained periods can damage the body in many ways. You can buy inexpensive measuring devices but

read the instructions carefully. Consult your doctor if you have any concern.

For other measures of general health you should consult your health service provider. These include but are not confined to:

- Cholesterol levels (known to contribute to risk of stroke and age heart disease).
- Basic metabolic rate (BMR) and age (if your BMR is higher than your calendar age you need to improve your metabolic rate). Increased exercise helps build healthy muscle tissue that improves your metabolic rate.
- Triglyceride levels.
- Metabolic age (if your metabolic age is higher than your calendar age it is an indication that you need to improve your metabolic rate). Increased exercise will build healthy muscle tissue that will improve your metabolic age.
- Glucose levels (can be checked to help diagnose diabetes).

Exercise tips

A twenty minute walk can improve your mood for a whole day. Our brains are still hard-wired to walk twelve miles a day, yet for many of us our lives at home and work are largely sedentary. Watching TV every night to relax can have the opposite effect by making you feel depressed, but the average American, for example, spends more time watching TV over their lifetime than in paid work. If you feel tired, exercise can help to refresh you. There are benefits to be had from owning and walking a dog—one study showed that dog owners are eight times more likely to be alive one year after a heart attack than people who do not own a dog.

The US Surgeon General in 2008 recommended that adults walk the equivalent of 10,000 steps per day to stay healthy. The real danger to your health and well-being comes when you average less than 5,000 steps a day. You can buy simple devices that do the counting for you—use these and other tools to help assess your own levels of activity, and try to incorporate natural exercise into your daily/ weekly routines. Global Corporate Challenge (www.gettheworld-moving.com) is designed to encourage organizations to compete by getting their employees to walk 10,000 steps over 120 days in teams of seven, thereby walking "around the world."

To stay fit, many people increasingly rely on planned aerobic training like going to the gym or cycling long distances at speed at weekends. This is efficient and beneficial but can add time pressures to already packed schedules—you do not need to go to the gym to stay reasonably fit. An alternative is to take advantage of opportunities for natural exercise—the exertion and energy associated with the everyday activities of a less sedentary life. Examples include walking or cycling short distances rather than using the car, carrying shopping bags rather than using trolleys, using manual tools in the garden or hobbies instead of power tools, using stairs rather than lifts (at least for some of the floors). Think of things you do routinely that you could transform into natural exercise by changing your mindset and how you do it. It is worth noting that frequent, short periods of moderate exercise are better for you than intense but irregular exercise.

To increase the level of physical activity in your life, consider these options:

30 minutes vigorous walking most days
Walk with others, make it a pleasure
Walk, cycle some all or of the way to work
3 x 30 minutes aerobic exercises per week
Use stairs wherever you can
Take up regular, rigorous activity of any kind
Get outdoors (walk, run, cycle, kayak, climb, sail)
Make, mend, fix, paint, decorate
Do the garden energetically—get rid of power tools
Stand up/walk away from your desk every 45 to 60 minutes—disengage mentally
Take up physical sports, make it fun
Get a dog and exercise it
Learn to dance

The US Department of Health has published very helpful physical activity guidelines that can be related to personal circumstances, age etc.[26] For the highly competitive, mobile apps can be very helpful.[27]

Lack of or poor quality sleep has multiple effects including irritability, reduced concentration, lower tolerance, emotionality, ill health, proneness to stress, etc. For most people the solutions are relatively straightforward. Most people need at least seven hours of quality sleep, and should go to sleep at a regular time, in darkened, quiet rooms. Some people need rituals to help them sleep better. Everything you ever wanted to know about sleep and sleeping better can be found through Stanford University's Sleep Research Center website.[28]

Good diet is essential to maintaining a healthy physical condition.[29] If the body receives all the nutrients it needs regularly it will be fit and strong for growth and its maintenance functions. A balanced diet helps you stay positive and energetic. Mind and body are closely integrated, so you are feeding your mind as well as your body. A balanced diet improves decision-making and problem-solving, and even the ability to remember things.

If someone makes tens of thousands of small, poor dietary choices (packets of crisps, butter, fatty foods, salt, fast and highly processed foods, alcohol, etc.) over a lifetime, these accumulate to have a major impact on their body, influencing the expression of their genes. Becoming overweight and unhealthy reduces energy and can seriously undermine resilience.

The World Health Organization (WHO) recommends:

- achieving a healthy weight and energy balance;
- limiting energy intake from fatty foods, shifting from saturated to unsaturated fats;
- increasing the consumption of fruits and vegetables, whole grains and nuts;
- limiting salt/sodium intake;
- limiting sugar intake;
- unbalanced diets have direct causal links to various forms of cancer, heart disease and strokes.

In discussing physical health, we have explored how poor sleep, an unhealthy diet and falling below a critical threshold of physical activity, all contribute to weakened resilience. Sleeping well, following a healthy diet and taking regular exercise all raise levels of well-being, but this is not necessarily the same as improving resilience for the long-term. Nevertheless, long-lasting benefits for personal resilience can be achieved by those who make sustained efforts to look after their physical condition, and who take advantage of situations and opportunities that challenge their endurance and help them to build physical toughness.

PURPOSEFULNESS

Core techniques: (i) spend time thinking about what really matters to you; (ii) set and pursue meaningful goals; (iii) bring mindfulness to your work.

Spend time thinking about what really matters to you

It often takes a crisis for people to step back and question what is really important to them, what they truly value and care about. Such crises are often life-changing, not only because of the stress and trauma involved, but because they can lead to a much clearer sense of purpose and an alignment of personal goals and values. When this is the case, those involved become more resilient through the process of finding meaning as a result of their difficulties. Others are better equipped from the start to cope with traumatic events in their lives, because they already have a strong sense of purpose and a firm belief system underpinning their resilience.

This underpinning may be based on belonging to an established religion, or to a community that shares an alternative faith. In either case, there is evidence for the well-being and resilience benefits of adhering to a faith that explains the origins of the universe, provides a code of ethics, a community life, and an explanation of life after death. Other people hold a more personal, less institutionalized, set of values and beliefs. As long as the belief system is clear and firmly held, it may be referred to as a "moral compass," or a "shatterproof set of beliefs," and there is good evidence to show that simply having such clarity and conviction boosts resilience.[30]

It seems likely that as a species we have inherited a genetic disposition to believe in things or something beyond ourselves that contributed to our survial as a species. The brain seems to be hard-wired for faith in some form or other.[31]

In his book *Spiritual Evolution: A Scientific Defence of Faith*, the emminent Harvard researcher George Vaillant argues that some of the positive emotions that we have evolved biologically over millions of years, especially love, hope, joy, forgiveness, faith, awe and gratitude, all underlie spirituality. They all in some way take the individual beyond a concern for him or herself. Vaillant notes that the brain structures that control positive emotions (the limbic system) evolved more recently and are physically separate from the brain structure controlling negative emotions (the hypothalamus, which is all about the self and short-term survival). He argues that spirituality comprises positive emotion and social connection. All the great religious traditions in the world throughout history have preached love and compassion as guiding principles.[32]

We take no view on the validity of religious or secular frameworks. We do support the individual's right to search for personal truth, self-knowledge, spirituality, meaning and purpose in life. There is substantial evidence that living a life guided by a moral code that is not harmful to, or intolerant of, others provides a sense of meaning and purpose that contributes to sustained resilience. Equally, the pursuit of goals that are not just about oneself but that also go beyond oneself, and are guided by strong personal values, leads to a sense of meaning and purpose and to sustaining resilience in the face of challenge or difficulty. Volunteering and contributing to the welfare of others have a strong link to both well-being and enduring resilience. Many companies support volunteering and community support activities. Johnson & Johnson, for example, has a policy for paid and unpaid leave for activities that support communities and make employees proud of the company they work for.

The overall message here is that it is worth taking active steps to clarify your values and work out what matters to you, rather than waiting for your resilience to be tested to the limit first. This is, however, another area where strengths can be "over-used"—if beliefs are held too rigidly they may lead to intolerance and even violence, and this lack of balance can undermine resilience in a number of ways, not least by damaging *Adaptability* and *Social Support*.

In the work context, this clarification exercise may take the form of identifying the kind of work that is deeply meaningful and satisfying to you, and even making a career change if this is very different to what you are currently doing. Edgar Schein's Career Anchors analysis has helped many people over the years, by helping them to identify

139

which of the seven anchors applies to them—in other words, which element needs to be a major part of their role in order for them to feel happy and satisfied at work. The anchors are:

- Pure Challenge;
- General Managerial Competence;
- Security/Stability;
- Technical/Functional Competence;
- Autonomy/Independence;
- Entrepreneurial Creativity;
- Service/Dedication to a Cause.

The power in the Career Anchors model is the idea that each person gets most of their career satisfaction and enjoyment from one of these anchors. So if your career anchor is Technical/Functional Competence but a series of promotions has meant that 90% of your current role requires the exercise of General Managerial Competence, you should probably consider making a change. Even if you get good feedback as a manager, you are unlikely to be happy and fulfilled at work if you have so little opportunity to exercise your Technical/Functional Competence. The Career Anchors Self-Assessment is available online from the publisher.[33]

There are, however, less drastic alternatives to changing career when you realize your role is out of line with what matters to you. In the case of your career anchor, there is often scope to shape your role to give you more scope to do what you really enjoy. Another angle is provided by the "Three Work Orientations" described below—a model that can help someone to view their job or career differently and shape it to provide a more positive experience. The question to ask yourself here is whether the work you do is just a job, a career, or a calling? People with a "job orientation" are not particularly excited about their work. Such people are typically seen as unmotivated, seeking their pleasure and satisfaction outside work. People with a "career orientation" are motivated both by the primary benefits of their work (such as income) and by its secondary benefits (such as social status). People with a "calling orientation" typically love and value what they do in and for itself.

Amy Wrzesniewski at New York University discovered, somewhat surprisingly, that in any given occupation, individuals may be found in the job, career, or calling orientation—for example, one person may have a "job orientation" towards their role as a nurse, while a colleague on the same team may see the role as a "calling."[34] Once again we see how the perceptions, beliefs and values that underpin resilience are specific, personal and even unique to the individual concerned.

How to develop *Purposefulness* and move from a job or career orientation into a calling is described in more detail in Chapter 7.

Setting and pursuing meaningful goals

Setting and pursuing meaningful goals for your life, participating in and contributing to associations and communities, and finding meaning and purpose in life are all closely related. All are powerful contributors to well-being and life satisfaction and the resilience that is associated with it.

As we have seen above, having clear and meaningful Life Goals is a major contributor to well-being. In the absence of goals people tend to flounder and their lives can feel pointless, which damages their resilience. Personal goals have an important role to play, as do the goals of the job and the organization you work for. We are the only the species on the planet that creates goals about future events and states. Goals are very important to human beings because they help render life meaningful and purposeful. Recent studies have shown that simply having goals can have as much value as achieving them.[35]

There are many benefits to having goals. They include:

- providing focus and a sense of journey;
- capturing what you want for yourself in the future;
- helping you to cope with life's upsets;
- energizing you;
- keeping you motivated;
- helping you review progress;
- enabling sharing and mutual support.

It has been recognized for a long time that a clear sense of purpose (or mission) is a significant factor in inspiring, motivating, and energizing people to be successful, often against the odds. This has been well-established in countless studies of organizational success.[36]

It is often said that, "People who do not know where they are going usually end up somewhere else." Many people remember the power of John F. Kennedy's vision in 1961: "I believe that this nation should commit itself to achieving the goal, before this decade is out, of landing a man on the moon and returning him safely to the Earth." And everyone remembers Martin Luther King's speech: "I have a dream..." More recent examples include Amazon.com's vision to be Earth's most customer-centric company; to build a place where people can come to find and discover anything they might want to buy online. Richard Branson has said of his plans for Virgin Galactic to be the first company in the world to send tourists into space: "If you don't dream nothing happens." He plans to establish a space hotel which people can use as a base and take tours on automated spacecraft to the Moon and back. Not all dreams need to be this grand but dreams are important to everyone. Dreams are the hopes, aspirations and wishes that are part of each person's identity and give purpose and meaning to life.

Goals need to be meaningful and personal to the individual. Some of the most powerful goals are about personal growth, connection to others, and contributing to others or making a difference. The more personally important goals are in terms of someone's core values the more they contribute to their well-being. On a more enduring basis, being guided by deeply held personal values is a key contributor to individual resilience.[37]

Kennon Sheldon at the University of Misouri has extensively investigated the importance of goals to people's lives. He identified two broad types of goals—*intrinsically satisfying* and *extrinsically satisfying* goals.[38]

According to Sheldon, intrinsically satisfying goals are valued for themselves as they are based on deep personal values. Progress towards them as well as achieving them can be deeply satisfying. By contrast, extrinsically satisfying goals are valued for what they lead to, which often involves comparing oneself with others in terms of appearance, popularity, possessions and status. These goals can be stressful and may not lead to fulfillment.

There are four broad categories of goals that are important to everyone:

- accomplishments (education, career, strengths);
- relationships (belonging, bonding, connecting);

- contributing (giving, making a difference, legacy);
- part of something bigger (religious, spiritual, humanity).

For each of these you should ask:

- What do I want from my life? In what way does my work help?
- What am I trying to achieve with my life?
- What would I like to have achieved when I look back over my life?
- What is really important to me?
- Where does my life satisfaction come from?

The next step is to start writing your personal goals. If they are not written down they are nothing more than ill-defined hopes and aspirations that change and fluctuate without you realizing it. Emmons offers this advice: try to express your goals positively. Make them things you want to achieve and do rather than things to avoid. Aim for things beyond your own sense of pleasure, things that involve others, contributing to or benefitting others. Plan to pursue your goals in a prudent, patient, and persevering manner, and finally appreciate and savor progress, and not just the end point.

Bringing mindfulness to your work

In its broadest sense being mindful is enjoying the present in terms of what is good, and experiencing the positive in whatever it is you are doing. Some people do this quite naturally and routinely, but it is a skill that can be learned and developed with practice. Savoring is a closely related practice. Mindfulness can range from a habit akin to savoring, to a fully fledged set of formal techniques and practices called mindfulness meditation. Meditation is one of the most powerful techniques we have for inducing relaxation and positive emotions.[39]

The habit of savoring helps many people to keep a sense of perspective in terms of what is important, and to take advantage of the learning that can be gained from daily experiences. There is convincing evidence that learning to appreciate present (or past) experience in a mindful way brings strong, positive effects, including increased optimism and lower levels of depression.[40]

Savouring focuses attention on what is good and enjoyable, however small, and helps people to turn things they dislike doing into things they derive pleasure from. For example, turning chores or disliked activities at work into something that one can feel more positive about can make a big difference. Things to consider are:

- Can it be systematised and done in a methodical manner?
- Can you turn it into a challenge, with goals and targets?
- Can you make it rhythmic?
- Can you increase your skill and efficiency in doing it?
- Can you involve others, make it more fun?
- Can you alter the tempo and concentrate on the physical sensations?

People who do not learn to appreciate and extract what is pleasing and good in the present, run the risk that days, months, years quickly go by unnoticed, unused, unappreciated. Learning to savor and appreciate the present, or even things one has disliked doing in the past, can even change the chemical balance in one's body to a more favorable profile.

The practical advice given in these two chapters is equally relevant to all our readers, and to the individuals you are seeking to support—whether CEO, function head, department manager, or any other employee of an organization. It forms the foundation for the design of workplace programs and other interventions intended to help individuals build their resilience. In the next chapter we focus directly on what managers and organizations as a whole can do to support individual resilience in the workplace.

CHAPTER 6

ORGANIZATIONAL APPROACHES: THE INDIVIDUAL AT WORK

RESILIENCE-BUILDING ACTIVITY AT THE INDIVIDUAL LEVEL

In this chapter and the next, we describe and discuss approaches to building resilience in the workplace. We believe the most effective approach is for organizations to incorporate resilience-building within an overall well-being or other change management strategy, and here we discuss the two main components of such a strategy, (i) resilience-focused training and development for individuals and (ii) good management practices and organizational strategies that help to build resilience on a wider level. In earlier chapters we commented on the impact of the constantly accelerating rate of technological change that affects both our work lives and our personal lives. Combined with ever-increasing pressures to perform, the need for high levels of resilience in the workforce has never been greater, if we are to ensure sustained health and success for individuals and the organizations they work in.

The first and foremost thing for busy and hard-pressed managers to understand is that their own resilience is critical to their effectiveness. Equally, the resilience of the people that a manager is responsible for, and interacts with, can be sustained or undermined by the manager's actions and behavior. Ultimately, however, the role of the manager and organization is a facilitative one—it is the individual who must take personal responsibility for improving their own resilience.

There are three broad approaches to supporting the resilience of all who work in an organization:

1. *Providing personal development for managers*: This enables the manager to act as a "resilient role model" for others,[1] and helps

the manager to behave constructively under pressure—reducing the risk of undermining the personal resilience of employees, e.g. through bullying, making unreasonable demands, or criticizing rather than supporting.

2. *Providing developmental support for building the resilience of employees* by facilitating enduring improvements in the personal resilience of employees, and creating a resilience-building opportunity that each employee needs to take personal responsibility for benefitting from.

3. *Promoting good management practices and strategy* throughout the organization, and ensuring that strategic plans and interventions are conducive to resilience-building.

In this chapter we discuss the first two approaches, and in Chapter 7 we cover the topic of general management practice and strategy.

SUPPORTING RESILIENCE DEVELOPMENT—WHAT ARE THE OPTIONS FOR MANAGERS?

What can the busy line manager do to support and build resilience in others? What provision can managers and organizations make for this kind of personal development? First, the manager needs to be aware that there are many things in the work environment that can undermine resilience and well-being. We described these in Chapters 2 and 3. Equally there are things a manager can do to help strengthen individual resilience both directly and indirectly.

There are essentially two ways of approaching resilience-building, one as a "response" to a defined problem such as crisis or perceived threat, and the other as a "proactive effort" to boost resilience and enhance effectiveness in the face of continuing challenges and pressure. Resilience-building is generally seen as providing a buffer to stress and to pressure, but it goes well beyond this to act as a performance enhancer that benefits individual, team, and organizational success. We will show in this and in the next chapter that the most powerful approach is not to raise resilience as an end in itself, but to use resilience to underpin, support, and enhance other performance goals, especially in difficult and challenging times.

Ten things people managers can do to build and sustain resilience

---

Resilience-focused interventions (Chapter 6)

Personal development for managers

1. Help managers to take responsibility for improving their personal resilience.
2. Provide support for managers in assessing and managing their leadership impact style.

Developmental support for building the resilience of individual employees

3. Put discussions about resilience on the agenda.
4. Support resilience-building through management conversations and coaching.
5. Run resilience-building workshops and development programs.

Good management practices that help to build resilience (Chapter 7)

Active management of the sources of workplace pressure and support, for example:

6. Actively build positive working relationships (Work Relationships).
7. Strengthen meaning in work roles (Job Conditions).
8. Give people a say in planning, decision-making, and problem-solving (Control).
9. Resolve problems and manage change through Appreciative Inquiry (Managing Change).
10. Manage through strengths.

PERSONAL DEVELOPMENT FOR MANAGERS

1. Taking responsibility as a manager for developing your own resilience

This is illustrated by the stories of Lynda and Matsuko.

Lynda's story: using personal resilience-building to help with extreme work and personal stress

Lynda had joined the senior management team a year ago as the Director of Operations. She acquired a new team. The atmosphere in both her own team and in the management team she had just joined was as she put it "horrible. I dreaded going to meetings. I was always in the role of harmonizer. I did not give my true opinions because there were so many explosions from other

---

147

people. Not only did I feel ineffective, it was painful for me. The behavior I was experiencing violated my core values. Confrontations between members of the team were aggressive and destructive. People cried, screamed, and walked out of meetings."

She felt she had reached the point of almost wanting to give up. "The demands were dragging me down and the hours were unsustainable. I would work from 8 am to midnight and then be in again for a meeting at 7 am. I was not sleeping enough, and I was gaining weight. I felt that despite all these hours I was not delivering what I needed to deliver. No-one told me. I could see it in the results."

In her new role Lynda had acquired additional responsibility for a department that for several years had been run by a former colleague of hers in an autocratic and controlling style that left the staff feeling very de-moralized. She tried to deal with the problems she encountered but it was very stressful. "I was giving too much of myself, assuming too much of the pain. I spent several months dealing with, seeing, and processing emotions that were not mine. I went on holiday and realized that I was putting my health, my family, and myself at risk."

She decided she needed to do something. Lynda volunteered to attend a resilience-building workshop that was supported by eight one-on-one coaching sessions. The workshop provided an understanding of the nature of resilience, and some basic tools but most importantly for her the insight that resilience can be built as a strength—rather than just being a remedial "sticking plaster." She saw this as a coming back rather than a bounce back.

In her coaching sessions, Lynda decided to work on and challenge her automatic negative thoughts, and at the same time build her confidence to intervene positively where she saw unacceptable behavior that went against her core values. During the coaching sessions she realized that for most of her life she was, as she put it, "attacking myself, nothing was ever good enough, and that I had been beating myself up for most of my life." She saw the resilience framework and practical tools she learned about in the workshop as a huge opportunity, as she put it, to look more realistically at what she had achieved.

This experience also impacted on her personal life. She was engaged to be married for the second time and was still hanging on to self-doubt and worrying about the commitment. She said to herself: "I am like everyone, I will do my best, 90% is good enough. I must not destroy it before I even try it. I need to give my new marriage as much or more respect as I seem to give my job."

In the management team, which is now functioning more positively, Lynda feels more able to give her views without worrying about them. She now raises issues when previously she would remain silent and she openly expresses disagreement as and when necessary, without shying away from conflict. She says it has become second nature to her. "It is how I behave at work."

The resilience tools that she found most helpful were disputing negative thoughts, using inquiry more than advocacy to discuss issues and also to resolve conflict, perspective-taking, using her natural strengths and creating rituals to limit the hours she spends at work. But overall, she says, "It is living and understanding the principles of resilience that makes the most difference. For me, it is a journey not an event."

Six months before we spoke, her resilience had been severely tested. Her husband was diagnosed with a malignant melanoma. "If I had not had these tools, and had not re-committed to myself that holiday, I would not have dealt with the news as I did. I felt, no matter what happens, I can deal with it, there is always hope however bad it looks. So I waited, researched, got organized and became emotionally present, and I would do whatever was needed." The tumor was eventually diagnosed as benign but there are still challenges ahead.

Finally, Lynda says that despite the challenges, frustrations, and stresses around her, she feels stronger to present her true self to others. She feels people respond differently to her as a manager, and as a result her resilience grows. As a manager she has held one-on-one discussions with members of her team and has discussed resilience issues with them and how she can support them.

Matsuko's story: using resilience-building to deal effectively with a challenging new role

Matsuko was a Department Manager in a major bank. Over a six-month period, Matsuko received six one-on-one coaching sessions specifically on her leadership style, with a particular focus on how she coped under pressure or when she was feeling stressed. Over the period she completed *Leadership Impact*, *i-resilience*, the MBTI, and Wave Professional Styles.[2]

One of her issues was anger-management. She could easily be provoked. She realized that when feeling stressed she could easily be moved to anger even with her own boss, resulting in her openly expressing views and opinions that she would later regret, or that caused damage to the relationship. She felt she lost credibility when this happened.

The coaching focused on using strengths rather than remedying weaknesses. As she put it, "I understand myself a lot better now. I am more conscious of the red flags, and instead of reacting negatively I use my strengths in relationship building and emotional intelligence to not only defuse the danger-points but to constructively build the relationship, so that the need to defuse a situation becomes less frequent. I have turned what was a weakness into a strength that I can build on. The emotional side of me is how I connect to and motivate people. It energizes me and others too." I feel stronger as a manager and more able to deal with pressures and what I used to see as provocations. The other benefit in her own words: "I am a convert to strengths-based management. Instead of feeling beset with problems all around me, I see opportunities to build on what is good, which I was often blind to because I worried so much about the insurmountable problems."

2. Assessing and managing your leadership impact style

It is well established that managers and leaders have a significant impact on whether employees feel happy and engaged, or stressed and burnt-out/disengaged. A detailed review of the research on this topic is provided by Ivan Robertson and Jill Flint-Taylor,[3] who developed the *Leadership Impact* framework and profiling tool.[4] As explained in more detail in Chapter 3, this tool uses the same models as the *i-resilience* questionnaire for assessing the individual (Five-Factor personality model) and the workplace situation (ASSET).

The Leadership Impact approach: In the case of *Leadership Impact*, the developmental report relates to the need for leaders to balance challenge with support. The report puts forward suggestions about how this is likely to play out in relation to the six ASSET sources of pressure and support, if the leader relies on his or her natural style. For example, the research indicates that leaders who are very confident in their own capability may have a negative impact on levels of well-being in the team—creating stress by failing to consult or take account of others' suggestions (the ASSET factor of *Control*). In terms of our earlier discussion on the relationship between well-being and resilience, this could be a temporary impact in some situations, but it could equally have an enduring effect on the personal resilience of some team members by undermining their confidence. The *Leadership Impact* analysis places particular importance on the "unintentional damage" that can be caused through the over-use of leadership strengths such as confidence, sense of duty, or concern for others.

The story of Fabio illustrates how a leader can flex his or her *Leadership Impact* style, with benefits for the resilience of those who report to him or her.

Fabio is a senior manager, heading up a large division in a multi-national company. He has a team of five direct reports, three of whom have been with him for several years, and two of whom joined the team eighteen months ago following the acquisition of another company. Until then, Fabio's 360° feedback had been consistently positive, with his colleagues and reports emphasizing their respect for his drive, determination, and tough negotiating skills. In subsequent review exercises, however, the scores from his direct reports were somewhat lower than he was used to seeing, especially in the areas of "Motivating Others" and "Managing Self." Some of the written comments included the words "unreasonable," "stubborn," and "aggressive," and during the review conversation with his manager, Aisha, she told him that she was troubled that she had even heard talk of his "bullying style." Aisha agreed with his suggestion that a difference in the cultures of the merged organizations might be a factor, as she recognized their organization had always had something of a reputation for tough, competitive leadership. However, she made it clear that she felt he needed to take responsibility for the impact he was having on his team.

At the time Fabio was part-way through an external leadership program, in which he had enrolled with a view to learning more about advanced strategic planning. He had turned down the option of 1:1 coaching offered by the program, but reflecting on the feedback and conversation with his manager, he decided to try a few sessions. At the outset, he completed a profiling exercise that included the *Leadership Impact* questionnaire.

Fabio was pleased to see that the report suggested his primary impact on the team was likely to encourage them to keep up momentum and to respond flexibly to changing requirements (the *Leadership Impact* style of *Pace*, i.e. providing positive, challenge pressure for the team by modeling, promoting, and rewarding fast-moving activity, flexible responding, change, ideas, enthusiasm, and creativity). The specific FFM traits underpinning this style were his inclination to challenge or ignore what he sees as unnecessary constraints, his personal energy and ability to maintain momentum, his proactivity and willingness to take the lead, and his general enthusiasm. In terms of the ASSET factors, his report suggested that he was likely to have a particularly positive impact on the management of *Job Security & Change*, and *Resources & Communication*.

He was, however, surprised by the suggestion that he could have a negative impact on the ASSET factor of *Control* (his reports' sense of feeling able to influence decisions and have their ideas listened to). The report had the following to say in this regard:

> "Your forceful, dominant style may prevent you from giving others sufficient opportunity to have their say, even when you recognize the need to involve them in plans and decisions. You are competitive and may be quite stubborn at times. It is important that you recognize when to compromise for the sake of gaining others' co-operation and enabling them to feel more in control of events."

On the same theme but in relation to the ASSET factor of *Work Relationships*, the report had this to say:

> "Reluctance to compromise may interfere with your ability to resolve conflict and create a climate of collaboration. If you behave aggressively, some may follow your example, while others will seek to minimize the risk of incurring your anger by limiting their involvement. If this happens, it will have a negative impact on creativity and innovation."

When he discussed this report and the situation at work with his coach, she introduced the idea of over-using certain leadership strengths, and the risks that this could create even at the most senior leadership levels. This insight helped him to understand that his high levels of personal energy and strong competitive streak had stood him in good stead for many years, helping him to earn his reputation for drive, determination, and tough negotiation. He had got to the point, however, where he was over-relying on his natural style, and defaulting to it even in those situations that required a less impatient, more accommodating approach. Although he was actually someone who took an active interest in the welfare of his team (something also highlighted in his *Leadership Impact* report), this was being masked by his assertive and sometimes even stubborn attitude—to the point where words like "bullying" were being used.

Fabio found it particularly useful to think about the problem as a risk to be managed—the risk of over-using what should really continue to be some of his most important leadership strengths. He signed up for the full course of coaching sessions, and with the help of his coach he improved his ability to flex his leadership style to suit a broader range of situations—and people. This had a noticeable effect on improving the general morale in the divisional leadership team. It also emerged later that his previous behavior had been undermining the *Confidence* of Ray, one of the new direct reports, to the point where it could very well have had an enduring negative effect on Ray's personal resilience. By understanding his impact on the team and learning to flex his style, Fabio has been able to make the best of his leadership strengths and increase the morale of his top team, as well as helping to rebuild Ray's confidence and avoid any long-term damage to his resilience.

While the *Leadership Impact* and *i-resilience* tools are specifically designed with workplace well-being and resilience in mind, there are other diagnostics to help assess and develop leadership style and these are included in our discussion.

An assessment tool that focuses specifically on the negative aspects of how a manager functions under pressure (sometimes called the "dark side" of leadership), is The Hogan Development Survey (HDS).[5] It identifies personality-based performance risks and "derailers" of interpersonal behavior when the individual is under pressure or is distracted. These derailers affect an individual's leadership style and actions. The HDS approach acknowledges that, under some circumstances, the derailers can actually be strengths. However, the focus is on what happens when these characteristics are over-used or taken to extremes, creating risks to performance and threats to good working relationships, and in extreme cases limiting careers.

The main scales on the HDS[6] are:

1. excitable: moody, easily annoyed, hard to please, and emotionally volatile;
2. skeptical: distrustful, cynical, sensitive to criticism, and focused on the negative;
3. cautious: unassertive, resistant to change, risk-averse, and slow to make decisions;
4. reserved: aloof, indifferent to the feelings of others, and uncommunicative;
5. leisurely: overtly cooperative, but privately irritable, stubborn, and uncooperative;

6. bold: overly self-confident, arrogant, with inflated feelings of self-worth;
7. mischievous: charming, risk-taking, limit-testing, and excitement-seeking;
8. colorful: dramatic, attention-seeking, interruptive, and poor listening skills;
9. imaginative: creative, but thinking and acting in unusual or eccentric ways;
10. diligent: meticulous, precise, hard to please, and tends to micromanage;
11. dutiful: eager to please and reluctant to act independently or against popular opinion.

We can see many of these derailers at work in the case of the "asshole" manager, also commonly referred to these days as a "toxic' leader or "psycho boss." Robert Sutton at Stanford University wrote a brief note in the Harvard Business Review Blog about his experience of what he called "asshole managers," and the damage they can do to morale and motivation. Within a few weeks he was inundated with thousands of messages of support, and endless examples of what people had experienced at the hands of such managers, and in no time at all the blog note had turned into a well-researched book.[7]

Sutton applies two tests he uses for spotting whether a person is behaving like a toxic manager:

Test One: After talking to the alleged toxic manager, does the "target" feel oppressed, humiliated, de-energized, or belittled by the person? In particular, does the target feel worse about him or herself?

Test Two: Does the alleged toxic manager aim his or her venom at people who are less powerful rather than at those people who are more powerful?

Toxic behavior includes personal insults, threats, and intimidation, both verbal and nonverbal, "sarcastic jokes" and "teasing" used as insult delivery systems, withering email flames, dirty looks, and treating people as if they are invisible. Sutton reports that much of this nastiness is directed by superiors to their subordinates (estimates run from 50% to 80%), with somewhat less between coworkers of roughly the same rank (estimates run from 20% to 50%), and "upward" nastiness—where underlings take on their superiors—occurs in less than 1% of cases.

Much of this behavior falls into the categories of "bullying" and "harassment," on which many companies take a stand and seek to discourage, but there is much of it that is accepted as just the culture of the organization, or just the boss's style. One of the consequences is humiliation, personal insecurity, and fear. Sutton quotes W. Edwards Deming, who concluded, long ago, "when fear rears its ugly head, people focus on protecting themselves, not on helping their organizations improve." Sutton also lists the many costs to an organization of tolerating toxic behavior, especially when bad behavior is tolerated, not addressed or even tacitly approved because the perpetrator is very senior or a star performer even when the bad behavior goes directly against espoused corporate values. These include damage to corporate reputation, distraction from core tasks because people try to protect themselves, reduced "psychological safety" and associated climate of fear, loss of motivation and energy at work, stress-induced psychological and physical illness, absenteeism, and the many other indicators of an unmotivated and disengaged workforce.

If toxic managers are seen to be tolerated or accommodated, the damage done to the morale and engagement of employees is magnified beyond the damage already done by rudeness, and other forms of offensiveness between colleagues. This often has an enduring impact on individuals as well—nothing saps resilience faster than being treated with a total lack of respect especially when double standards are at play.

Bad behavior, or its tolerance, or double standards in relation to the bad behavior of managers and high performers, is likely to undermine seriously the resilience and morale of those who experience or witness it. By contrast playing to one's strengths as an individual can have the opposite effect. The *Leadership Impact* approach emphasizes strengths rather than weaknesses or "dark side" characteristics, but makes it very clear that strengths can become derailers if over-used. The Myers Briggs Type Indicator (MBTI) uses a somewhat different approach. This focuses on personal style with an emphasis on what comes naturally to the individual, and pre-dates the strengths approach, which we discuss below, by several decades.[8]

We expect that many readers will be familiar with the MBTI, as this tool is widely used in leadership development. Those who are unfamiliar with the model should refer to the classic text by Myers and Myers for more detail.[9] Using the terminology introduced in this text, if you are already confident that you have established your Best-Fit Type, you should consider what stresses are associated with your MBTI Type, and as a result be mindful of falling into traps. For example, it is well established that SJ types, sometimes called "Thoughtful Realists," become stressed by uncertainty, change, and missed deadlines. By contrast, NT types, also known as "Thoughtful Innovators," are less stressed by these things. They are more likely to be stressed by routine, bureaucracy, and tight structure. The real challenge for the people manager is not to remedy the defects, but instead to play to their natural strengths. STs tend to be strong on the facts and efficiencies, whereas NTs are stronger on possibilities and strategy, unless of course they have learned compensatory skills.[10]

There are many leadership models that are relevant to the quest for a balanced and constructive leadership style. The work of Bob Kaplan and Rob Kaiser[11] is particularly useful for practical suggestions on how to make the most of your strengths by flexing your natural style.

DEVELOPMENTAL SUPPORT FOR INDIVIDUAL EMPLOYEES

Put discussions about resilience on the agenda

There is often reluctance and resistance to holding open and frank discussions on the subject of resilience in the workplace. Resilience and the potential harmful effects of sustained pressure of work should be a topic that is discussed and reviewed. It may feel uncomfortable at first but it becomes easier over time. To talk about the importance of resilience is not a sign of weakness or a subject to be avoided. Resilience is a strength that can be utilized to help people cope with pressure and the stressful demands of work. More than that, resilience enables people to thrive and enjoy themselves even under demanding conditions, and also to recover more quickly from setbacks. Almost everyone can benefit from increasing resilience. Because this is not always well understood, just raising the issue and having an open discussion can have beneficial effects.

There is a real benefit to managers who are prepared to openly discuss resilience because it demonstrates to their teams and direct reports that they care, not just about performance, but about how people feel. The single highest driver of engagement at work, according to a study conducted by Towers Watson, is whether employees feel that their managers are genuinely interested in their well-being. Less than 40% of workers in the study felt that their managers genuinely cared about their well-being.[12]

A useful way into discussing the topic is to invite team members to think of the benefits that might come to them if they could boost their resilience both in the work environment and at home. The responses usually cluster around avoiding stress, increasing effectiveness and getting more satisfaction from work and life as a whole. In addition or as a starting point, the manager can offer team members the chance to complete a personal resilience question-naire such as *i-resilience*[13] or the Ashridge Resilience Questionnaire (ARQ).[14] Constructive discussions can then take place about changes that would help people cope with pressure, and deliver results under demanding conditions without becoming stressed or burning out.

Support resilience-building through management conversations and coaching

Much can be achieved in the everyday work context by setting a good example, and acknowledging when things are tough both for you as a manager and for members of your team. Be prepared to take the opportunity, in performance reviews, coaching sessions, and informal discussions, to make practical suggestions such as those described in Chapters 4 and 5. It is important to focus on resilience as a strength to be built and not as a sign of weakness. The benefits of increasing personal resilience should be stressed. Next we tell the story how a function head in a major bank used resilience-building to help successfully integrate three teams, following a re-organization of the business.

Eric's story: using resilience-building to integrate three new teams

Eric is a senior executive in a financial services organization, who was respon-sible for the Wealth Management Division, an assortment of business units and companies ranging from asset management to life insurance. He had attended a one-day seminar on resilience-building, and opted for one-on-one coaching, deciding that a resilience focus was the missing element he had been looking for.

He had inherited a new team, following a re-structuring in the bank, which brought several functions and business units together for the first time under his leadership. There was a feeling of discomfort, loss of autonomy, old rivalries, and a deep suspicion that the new structure would not work. Most of the new team felt pessimistic about the changes, and the economic climate in which they were doing business was the worst it had been in decades. Eric had indeed taken on the leadership of a gloomy, fearful, and resentful team of senior managers, who each led similarly fearful and gloomy teams.

Eric was looking for a common denominator that would unite the managers responsible for his new portfolio of businesses. It was unlikely to be loyalty to the umbrella organization in which they were a major part, because like many banks at the time it too was in a state of crisis. Eric believed that you could typically galvanize a disunited team to act collaboratively, if they felt the heat of a burning platform or they were facing an exciting new opportunity. Neither was true in this case, as the business units were profitable and stable even though the bank that owned them was facing severe difficulties. He felt he needed something else to bond the team emotionally.

All the members of the new team were dealing with a lot of pressure in their professional lives and many also in their personal lives. He decided to offer help and support on resilience-building, which would result in both individual and personal advantage as well as corporate advantage. Through a series of meetings and a workshop, followed by one-on-one discussions, Eric says he "catapulted the team through the initial forming and norming stages of team building." The focus on resilience brought the team together and built trust because of the openness required when talking about and building resilience. The members of the team showed trust and discussed their own vulnerabilities early on within the framework of building resilience, and they shared experiences of dealing with worries, fears, and uncertainties.

As Eric put it, "There was a significant reduction in male testosterone and ego-driven tendencies, less vying with each other, less competitiveness, resulting in better discussions, better decision-making, and less defensiveness." The focus on resilience allowed him to see a new side of the people who worked with him, and he also noticed an increased readiness to take on other people's views. The benefits to the team have endured over a turbulent three-year period. "We feel like a team running a marathon together." We all recognized that we were part of a professional and personal support system.

In personal terms, Eric feels the resilience focus gave him a better understanding of the people in his team, more so than outdoor team-building events. He feels it brought the relationship between him and the new direct reports closer, and helped narrow the gap more quickly between the new managers and the longer established members of his team. For him, the ongoing benefit was "an underlying awareness, almost subliminal, like practical philosophy, use it when you need it. It helps to know it is there."

He concludes: "The individual resilience focus resonates with people, who feel more supported in difficult times, it exposes our frailties but builds us and makes us stronger at the same time. It reminds us of the need for balance in our lives, and how to get it. It helped me cope with two job changes in three years, and three children under the age of four. It just supports me. I am able to have clear conversations in the middle of a stressful day."

Run resilience-building workshops and development programs

There are basically two approaches to formal resilience-training and development interventions—the *direct* and the *indirect*. The approaches of Hay Group and the Hardiness Institute are examples of the *direct approach*, where the prime focus is on developing habits of thought and behaviors that help the individual deal effectively with challenging circumstances, adversity, and emotional set-backs.

Hay Group's[15] *approach* to developing personal resilience is based on (i) building skills to analyze beliefs, in order to develop awareness of how these beliefs can affect personal resilience, (ii) the skill of calming yourself and focusing in the present, and (iii) skills to change your beliefs that can undermine your resilience. The Hay approach also makes a useful distinction between skills which require some time commitment, and "fast skills" which can be applied to boost resilience in the moment. The development focuses on seven skills to boost resilience:[16]

1. ABC—learning the connection between your "in the moment" thoughts and beliefs and behavioral and emotional consequences of adversity;
2. Thinking traps—recognizing the errors in thinking we are often unaware of, for example, jumping to conclusions;
3. Detecting icebergs—building an awareness of the deep-seated beliefs we have of how the world works and how this can impact upon our emotions and behavior;
4. Calming and focusing—finding ways to step back from adversity, create breathing space and think more resiliently;

5. Challenging beliefs—a process by which the breadth and thus accuracy of our understanding of events can be enhanced, leading to more effective and sustained problem-solving behaviors;
6. Putting it in perspective—learning to stop the spiraling of catastrophic thinking and turn it into realistic thinking;
7. Real-time resilience—putting it all into practice in the moment; this skill is reliant on mastering the others and offers a "fast skill" which does not rely on having the time to think through a resilience reaction in depth.

These skills were originally identified and incorporated into the Penn Resilience Program, a highly successful and much emulated school-based intervention designed to reduce depression among young people. They were also incorporated into the US Army Master Resilience Training that we describe in more detail later in the next chapter. The University of London resilience-training studies, referred to earlier, also had much in common with the cognitive or "re-framing" emphasis of these programs.

The training provided by the Hardiness Institute[17] is based on a twelve-year longitudinal research project inside one large organization, spanning many years, in which the characteristics of people who coped with and thrived on a period of sustained organizational uncertainty and change were compared with those people who in identical circumstances succumbed to stress and other problems. As we outlined in Chapter 1, the researchers identified three resilient attitudes which they labeled Commitment, Control, and Challenge: "If you are strong in the 3Cs, you believe that, as times get tough, it is best for you to stay involved with the people and events around you (commitment) rather than to pull out, to keep trying to influence the outcomes in which you are involved (control) rather than to give up, and to try to discover how you and others can grow through the stress (challenge) rather than to bemoan your fate."[18] The researchers concluded that it is the combination of hardy attitudes and skills that help people survive and thrive under stress conditions. The courage and motivation of the three resilient attitudes help bring about the skills of transformational coping and social support. The Institute also offers a test of stress management and coping resilience that evaluates individual and organizational resources for effectively managing stressful changes.

By contrast, the *indirect approach* is to include these skills and habits within a wider framework that boosts the overall effectiveness of the individual in two ways. Firstly, this approach helps to buffer and protect people from the harmful effects of setbacks, and strengthens their ability to deal with adversity. Secondly, it enables them to thrive and perform at their best by building on strengths and by increasing positive emotion—among other things, as we outlined in Chapters 4 and 5. The wider framework also includes the physical and biological foundations (physical activity, sleep, and nutrition), and the emotional, social, cognitive, and spiritual dimensions which we described earlier from the perspective of the individual.

Next we tell the story of how voluntary lunchtime seminars, designed to give insights into personal resilience-building, gradually grew to have far-reaching impact across the organization.

From lunchtime seminars to a senior executive development program

It all started with a chance meeting in 2008 between one of the authors and a former colleague who worked in a senior leadership and development role for a large international bio-technology company. He said his company was looking for ways to help people deal with the considerable pressures they were under, especially in the light of a major problem caused by a supply-chain failure that had caused patient hardship and considerable distress for everyone involved. He described it as "quite a dark period" for the company and for himself. In addition to the medical supply problem, a merger was pending, his own boss had left, and his future was unclear.

He said that one of the Global HR priorities was Leading in Challenging Times. Senior leaders were experiencing ever greater pressure and yet the HR function was not offering anything practical or concrete to help leaders perform consistently, despite the array of pressures on them. The company was young, and the founder was fearful of letting go of the entrepreneurial spirit that had driven success in the past. Despite the pressures of launching new products, constant demands to lower costs, and a series of acquisitions—to say nothing of the economic collapse a few years earlier, and external market pressures—managers were expected to be self-sufficient and to cope. Up till that time, the company had experienced only rapid growth.

The external and internal pressures on employees, to recover from the supply chain failure and to sustain supplies, were extreme. The company had

---

piloted a workshop on managing energy not time[19] and the learning and organization development (L&OD) specialist had been looking for new ways to provide support. On learning about resilience-building workshops that lasted anywhere between a half-day and two days, he asked what could be done in a lunch-break of say 90 minutes, which could be offered to employees on a voluntary basis. He said he did not want to add to the pressure people were under and did not want to distract them from their work.

This was a challenge that was hard to resist, and a 90-minute workshop was designed and trialed in Holland and the UK. The workshop, which was positioned as a taster of things employees could do to self-manage and boost their resilience, covered the physical and biological foundations, the role of positive emotions, the benefits of working with strengths and getting into flow, the value of optimism, challenging negative thoughts, and the role of meaning to help deal with hardship and ongoing challenges. The initial evaluations were very positive and the main message was that the workshop needed to be longer, providing more time for discussion and sharing, but also the opportunity to experience the practical tools rather than just learn about them.

A half-day version called Building Your Resilience was developed, and then a full-day version. The Workshops were run in a variety of countries, including various parts of Europe, the USA, Canada, and Brazil. A significant finding was that the material in the resilience training did not need to be adapted for different cultural groups, though translations of some key words and phrases were provided from time to time. The workshops were run at sales conferences, and also as one-and-a-half day workshops for specific management teams. The first day focused on individuals in the context of their lives as a whole, while the second day was devoted to discussion of the implications for their roles as managers and as members of a leadership team. Throughout, the focus was on boosting the resilience of the individual in the context in which he or she was working.

Additional voluntary workshops were developed called Sustaining Your Resilience, as a follow-up to the Building Resilience Workshops. A Resilience Workshop for Managers was also developed where the focus was on what managers can do to support and sustain resilience in the workspace. The workshops evolved over an eighteen-month period, during which the company became subject to a takeover bid, which eventually took place. The takeover only added to the stress levels being experienced. The demand for the workshops grew as the company seemed to experience one trauma after another.

The acquiring company was interested in the use of resilience-building as a mechanism, not only to help people deal with challenging times but also to help people perform at their best. Resilience was no longer seen as a remedial quality in response to a problem, but more as an asset to build and enable people to thrive. It had become acceptable and normal to talk about resilience.

Resilience training is now integrated into the company's six-month Regional Leadership Development Program for High Potentials, run around the world in conjunction with the Harvard Business School. Over a thousand people have passed through the program. Resilience has at last arrived as a corporate value and behavior to be developed and rewarded.

Evaluations revealed that the impact of the training was highly personal. The resilience training was an integral part of a change program and participants took out of it what they saw as being most helpful to them both as a person and as a manager. The combined approach enabled them to think how best to become more effective in challenging times in their lives as a whole, and also as a manager of a team during a period of tremendous change and uncertainty that had become the norm rather than the exception. The L&OD specialist commented: "Resilience is now seen as a key contributor to sustained performance by helping people manage themselves in difficult times."

CHAPTER 7

ORGANIZATIONAL INTERVENTIONS: THE WORKPLACE SITUATION

MANAGING THE SOURCES OF WORKPLACE PRESSURE AND SUPPORT

Managing the sources of workplace pressure and support effectively, means balancing challenge pressure with support to create high levels of well-being, and taking action to fill the "well-being reservoir" so that individuals and teams are in a better position to cope with the pressures they face at the time. There is also no doubt that sustained good management of these factors—*Resources & Communication, Work Relationships, Control* etc.—has the potential to improve the resilience of individuals for the long-term e.g. by providing stretching goals backed up with appropriate levels of support.

Here we emphasize again the need to differentiate between the distinct but closely inter-connected concepts of personal resilience and well-being. Effective management of the sources of workplace pressure and support (the ASSET factors referred to in earlier chapters) will make it easier for individuals and the team to cope with pressure and recover from setbacks. We know this from the research showing that we all manage pressure better when we are healthy and feel good than when we are feeling drained and unfit. This improved management of pressure may last only as long as high levels of well-being are maintained, or it may translate into long-lasting improvements in personal resilience for individual team members.

The question here is what happens if changing circumstances—or a change of manager—tip the balance towards the factors draining well-being? What happens if an individual leaves the team and moves to another where the sources of pressure and support are not managed as effectively? The answer is that high levels of well-being in the team do not necessarily build the personal resilience of individual team members for the long-term, even though they enable those individuals to cope better with pressure in the short-term. Improving current well-being is not the same thing as building enduring personal resilience. Nevertheless, many of the specific actions taken by managers to improve workplace well-being and performance also have the potential to build the personal resilience of employees for the long-term. An example would be the provision of stretching goals, as mentioned above.

More generally, to achieve high levels of well-being in the team a manager needs to balance challenge pressure with support—not only in terms of his or her own management style, but also through the management of resources and other external factors. It is not difficult to see how the confidence and capability of individual team members are likely to grow under these conditions, boosting their personal resilience—although whether this actually happens depends on the interactions described in Figure 7.1.

In our discussion below, we include the role played by high levels of well-being in the work environment. It must, however, be borne

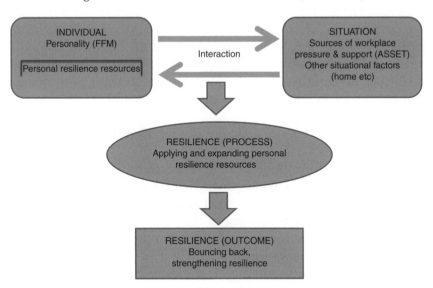

Figure 7.1   **Framework for understanding employees' resilience to workplace pressures**

165

in mind that the enduring benefits for personal resilience derive from specific actions or conditions that boost an individual's *Confidence, Adaptability, Social Support* skills and/or *Purposefulness*. High levels of well-being in the team do not necessarily lead to gains in personal resilience that endure when the individual's work situation changes.

We saw in Chapters 4 and 5 that there is a lot the individual can do to assess and build their own resilience, both directly and indirectly. There is no simple formula. Resilience like so many psychological constructs is the result of many different factors working together or undermining each other. We also saw in the earlier chapters that resilience at work overlaps with resilience in the rest of one's life. They cannot be separated or regarded as separate. Organizational practices and culture as well as leadership behavior can seriously undermine resilience. Equally, they can help boost and sustain the resilience of all members of an organization. Ultimately the individual should take charge of his or her own resilience as it affects their lives as a whole but there is a great deal that individual managers and those in leadership roles can do to boost resilience, directly or indirectly.

Below we look at a number of specific examples of how effective management of the six main sources of workplace pressure and support (the ASSET factors) can play a part in developing personal resilience for the long-term, as well as generating high levels of well-being in the short-term. The approaches we discuss here all have particular value for resilience building, as well as being more generally recognized as good management and leadership practices.

Work relationships: actively build positive working relationships

Some managers spend time and effort on creating positive relationships within the team, while others neglect this to focus on tasks, deadlines, and other "hard" objectives. In the ASSET framework, *Work Relationships* represents one of the six main sources of pressure or support. Relationships also appear under other factors—for example in the need for involvement and consultation (*Control*) and the importance of good communication (*Resources & Communication*). Good work relationships and team working can also have an enduring effect on various aspects of personal resilience, such as *Social Support* and *Confidence*.

The Positivity Ratio that we described in Chapter 4 also applies to individuals operating in teams, groups and, by implication, to whole organizations. Teams become more expansive, cooperative, productive and creative when their ratio of positive to negative emotions exceeeds 3 to 1. A landmark study published in 2005 showed that there are four critical ratios that successful business teams need to get right in order to perform at their best.[1]

1. The ratio of positive to negative communications within the team. Positive included support, encouragement, and appreciation while negative included disapproval, sarcasm, and cynicism.
2. The balance between Inquiry (exploring, examining) and Advocacy (arguing for or against) in team discussions.
3. The balance between external and internal reference, and
4. The connectivity within the team (cliques versus all together).

In the study, the leadership teams of 60 separate business units were divided into High Performing (N=15), Medium Performing (N=26), and Low Performing (N=19) groups, which were then observed having normal business disussions. The researchers found that the group of Top Performing teams had between 3 and 5 times as much positive as negative communication creating an expansive rather than restrictive atmosphere, whereas Low Performing teams had much more negative than positive communication. In Top Performing teams Advocacy and Inquiry were balanced, whereas in Low Performing teams there was much more Advocacy than Inquiry. Inward and outward focus was balanced in High Perfoming teams, but there was much more inward than outward focus in Low Performing teams. Finally, in terms of interpersonal connectivity, High Performing teams pulled together whilst Low Performing teams were very divided.

Generally, "calmer respectful" managers who do not unreasonably pressurize others and who do not engage in defensiveness, rude behavior or play politics at the expense of what really matters to people have engaged and motivated people around them who only need appropriate support and development, and a sense of meaning or purpose, to be at their best. Unfortunately, many managers when they come under sustained pressure themselves, become tense and indulge in negative behaviors that encourage negative behaviors in others, triggering a downward spiral caused by mutual blame. This is the negativity spiral we described in Chapter 4, and it relates to the need for managers to build their own resilience and manage their style and impact. To break the negativity spiral, the best way to begin is by increasing one's own positivity, then to increase others' positive experience of you, working in this way towards the upward spiral.

Job conditions: strengthen meaning in work roles

It is in the nature of human beings to want to be part of something they can believe in, and this relates directly to the resilience component of *Purposefulness* and to the ASSET factor of *Job Conditions*. In this context, "meaning" usually refers to something desirable to be achieved in the future that leads to a feeling of pride or part of an activity or service to others that is also a source of pride. Unfortunately, for many people work is a treadmill, a necessary evil that has to borne as a means to creating money on which to live and avoid boredom. We spend a great deal of our adult lives at work so it is a sadness that so few people really love their work. One option is to find better or more satisfying work, but that is not an easy option. The other option is to find meaning in what you do, or as a people manager to help others find more meaning in what they do. A Gallup Survey in 2010, revealed that only 20% of people say they like their work "very much" but the majority do not get a great deal of satisfaction from their work.[2]

In Chapter 5, we described Amy Wrzesniewski's research finding that in any given occupation, people can be in the job, career, or calling orientation. The Center for Positive Organizational Scholarship at the University of Michigan Ross School of Business, has developed a process and support materials called Job Crafting. The process captures "the active changes employees can make to their own job designs in ways that produce numerous positive outcomes, including engagement, job satisfaction, resilience, and thriving."[3]

Job crafting is a positive deviation from the traditional top-down processes of managers designing jobs for their employees. Job crafting "allows employees to utilize opportunities to customize their jobs to better fit their motives, strengths and passions." They can do this in three ways. They can alter the boundaries of their jobs, expanding or diminishing the scope of tasks, or changing how they perform tasks. Secondly, job crafters can change their relationships at work by altering the nature or extent of their interactions with other people. Thirdly, they can change how the job is construed, in terms of the role it plays in a wider context.

The classic example of the third approach is the hospital janitor who takes pride in his or her work, and derives satisfaction from developing positive work relationships and from actively contributing to the overall welfare of patients and the smooth running of the hospital, rather than seeing the role as a menial task of cleaning floors and emptying bins. The researchers report that "crafting" is a complex process that goes on informally over periods of time. (A distinction needs to be made between positive crafting and informal negative crafting which leads to lowered standards and compromise.) When sanctioned and supported, Job Crafting allows increased control, more meaningful interactions with others who benefit from one's work, the opportunity to feel passion, and an ability to cope with adversity at work. These seem to be both motivations to craft as well as desired outcomes. Documented outcomes from Job Crafting include changes in the meaning of work, and one's work identity, a sense of increased competence, personal growth, and ability to cope with future adversity.

As Amy Wrzesniewski and her colleagues have suggested, Job Crafting is a natural process that some employees engage in to find what is meaningful and satisfying in the roles they play. It is fundamentally about resourcefulness. Tasks and interpersonal relationships that make up a job are a "flexible set of building blocks that can be reorganized, restructured, and reframed to construct a customized job" that gives meaning, purpose and a sense of engagement to the job holder. It appeals to their sense of autonomy and freedom and desire to act in positive responsible ways. In some ways it is akin to the technique of Appreciative Inquiry that we describe below.

The Center for Positive Organizational Scholarship has developed a Job Crafting Exercise[4] that can be used on its own, or with others in a workshop, in one-on-one coaching or in classroom settings. Their website offers detailed guidance and support for each of these contexts.

Control: give people a say in planning, decision-making and problem-solving

Job Crafting and similar techniques provide one way of helping people to feel more in control of their environment and what happens to them at work. However, the most important way of achieving this is for managers to involve and consult those who report to them on a regular basis, as part of the everyday interaction within the team. This does not mean that every member of staff expects or needs to be consulted and to have their views taken into account at all times—that would be impractical and would make little sense. It does mean, however, that managers should develop good habits such as routinely asking the less assertive members of the team what they think, taking care not to dominate discussions, making sure people are generally informed about plans, and so on. Managers who are particularly forceful, dominant, confident and/ or decisive, need to be especially careful to ensure that they do not move ahead on decisions too quickly, or end up doing what they thought best in the first place without properly considering others' suggestions.

Apart from improving morale and reducing the short-term risk of stress in the team, giving people a say can build individual resilience for the long-term by encouraging them to stretch their capabilities (*Confidence*), engage more actively with others (*Social Support*), shape their roles and objectives (*Purposefulness*) and generate new ideas and approaches (*Adaptability*).

Change: resolve problems and manage change through Appreciative Inquiry

Managing change through Appreciative Inquiry, energizes and excites people about change which they feel themselves to be part of because they are involved in creating the way forward. Instead of change being a source of worry and stress, and managed top down, Appreciative Inquiry unleashes positive energy and enhances resilience.

David Cooperrider & Leslie Sekerka[5] define Appreciative Inquiry as

> a particular way of asking questions and envisioning the future that fosters positive relationships and builds on the basic goodness in a person, a situation, or an organization. In so doing, it enhances a system's capacity for collaboration and change. Discovering the best of the organization and its membership to ascertain what gives vitality to its members and the organization as a whole.

A useful in-depth handbook providing detailed practical guidance can be found in Whitney & Trosten-Bloom.[6] As the authors put it, the book explores "the transformational power of positivity and the kind of change that happens when strength touches strength, and one person's hope connects with another's hope." They see the task of leadership as to create an alignment of strengths in ways that make a system's weaknesses irrelevant.

Appreciative inquiry represents a mindset shift:

FROM	TO
Thinking about what is lacking	Recognizing the good that is there
Focusing on what is wrong	Seeing what works, what is right
Sticking with the past	Creating a future
Building on what has been	Creating new opportunities
Enforcing rules	Expanding opportunities
Reactive thinking	Proactive thinking
Convergent	Divergent

Appreciative Inquiry usually follows a sequence of distinct phases, often captured in the 4 Ds—*Discover, Dream, Design* and *Destiny*. These are described in depth with detailed practical guidance by Whitney and Trosten-Bloom.

Discovery is an extensive, cooperative search to understand the "best of what is and what has been."

Dream is an energizing exploration of "what might be." This phase is a time for people to collectively explore hopes and dreams for their work, their working relationships, their organization, and the world.

Design is a set of Provocative Propositions, which are statements describing the ideal organization, or "what should be." Design activities are conducted in large-group forums or within a small team.

Destiny is a series of inspired actions that support ongoing learning and innovation, or "what will be." This is the final phase of the 4-D Cycle.

A typical sequence for Appreciative Inquiry is like the following:

- Choose the positive as the focus of inquiry.
- Inquire into stories of life-giving forces.
- Locate themes that appear in the stories and select topics for further inquiry.
- Create shared images for a preferred future.
- Find innovative ways to create that future.

It is not our intention to provide a primer on Appreciative Inquiry, but rather to make the point that the process produces enduring change in a way that excites rather than drains people, thus sustaining and increasing resilience. We offer below the story of a modest inquiry that had a disproportionate positive impact on a de-moralized and fearful workforce.

Appreciative Inquiry as catalyst in motivating a positive approach to change

As part of a transformation strategy which had resilience-building as a key driver, the leadership team of a manufacturing site initiated an Appreciative Inquiry to help create a more positive future after several years of uncertainty, relentless change, downsizing and major disruption, which had left the site tired, frustrated and fearful not only for jobs but for the survival of the site as a whole.

Twenty people from all parts of the site, but not the leadership team itself, were nominated to be champions of the appreciative inquiry. They were briefed in a one-day workshop about Appreciative Inquiry and invited to agree the questions they wanted to ask, and to plan the data-gathering to cover as close as possible everyone on the site over a three-week period, which was quite a challenge as the site ran three eight-hour shifts a day.

The group decided that the aim of the Inquiry was to discover the best and reveal the best of the site and its people and to ascertain what creates energy, passion and commitment across the site. This was a clear break from the past where all surveys and inquiries had been controlled and run by others and focused on problems, mistakes and things that had gone wrong.

The Champions' briefing to the site was as follows:

We are doing an Inquiry, which involves everyone on the site, to focus on what we do best and find ways to do more of it, and make this site a great place to work. It is different because it focuses solely on what we do well in order to create an environment for positive change that everyone can buy into. We have designed, and will carry out the Inquiry ourselves, will process the results ourselves and engage in a dialog with the leadership team about what they and we can do.

This benefits you by making you more appreciated, less stressed, and your role more rewarding and fulfilling. Please come to our discussions. Together we can build a future we can all believe in. We are inviting everyone on the site to come to meetings lasting an hour in small groups and we will be asking only four questions.

1. What would it look/feel like for this site to be a great place to work?
2. Focusing on what already works well, give us some examples from your experience of where this happens and tell us what was it made you feel good about it?
3. Can you think how we can make examples like these more of an everyday occurrence?
4. How do you think the leadership team should support the implementation of our ideas?

After the meetings, which will take place over the next two to three weeks we will be processing your answers, to find common themes to quickly implement change that the whole site will buy into. We will share the findings with the site and seek feedback before we discuss next steps with the site leadership team. This is a real opportunity for us to help identify and implement the kinds of change that will make us not only a high-performing site but also a great place to work.

Despite considerable logistical difficulties, the champions managed to talk to 95% of the site, which was virtually everyone given absences due to sicknesses, holidays, and work assignments elsewhere. They had planned to have 60 meetings in a three-week period. It was a heroic effort. The champions then met as a group, and were facilitated by an external consultant to distill the data into core messages to share with the site as a whole and discuss with the site leadership team.

The findings were expressed in the direct and dignified language that is often the case with Appreciative Inquiry, and were displayed on posters across the site, inviting comment and reactions, before opening up a constructive dialogue with the leadership team.

One result of the ensuing dialogue was the first ever one-day offsite meeting between the senior management team and the second level of supervisors and people managers, to discuss as equals the way forward to ensure not only that the site would survive closure, but also that it would be competitive in world terms and, even better, a great place to work. A decision was made to rename the group the extended site leadership team, instead of having two groups called the site leadership and the second level leadership. The unifying experience was inspiring, and the positive energy released was palpable, with smiles and warmth and enthusiasm where previously there had been defensiveness, cynicism, suspicion. The extended leadership team agreed to a quarterly one-day offsite meeting to exchange ideas and review progress. The Appreciative Inquiry had made the emotional change possible, and significantly boosted morale and engagement across the site. The mood changed from pessimism to realistic optimism, with follow-up evaluations indicating longer-term resilience gains for individuals.

STRENGTHS-BASED MANAGEMENT

In Chapter 5 we described the benefits of identifying individual strengths and finding new and different ways to utilize your strengths both in the current work role and in other areas of life. Here we look at the case for managing through strengths rather than focusing primarily on remedying and eliminating weaknesses to maximize performance at work. This approach is particularly relevant for the development of *Confidence* and *Adaptability*.

Much has been written on the subject of strengths-based leadership and the benefits of focusing on and harnessing strengths[7] and the Gallup Organization has played a pioneering role in raising awareness and providing practical tools to the attention of both managers and people in general. The argument for focusing more on strengths and less on weaknesses is that everyone has strengths, developed or latent, that we are more motivated and energized when working with our strengths, and that the greatest potential for growth lies in using our strengths rather than remedying our weaknesses. By using our strengths we feel authentic, real, and fulfilled. Making the most of our strengths helps us cope with or compensate for our weaknesses. From the resilience perspective, working with our strengths is energizing not draining and as a result we resist burnout and recover more quickly.

The Centre for Applied Positive Psychology (CAPP),[8] one of the leading centers of expertise on strengths-based working, has identified ten business benefits. CAPP argues that focusing more on strengths helps the organization:[9]

1. Tap into unused talent throughout the organization. Too much time is spent attempting to improve the performance of people while less attention is paid to getting the best out of them.
2. Attract and retain more of the people it needs. People enjoy and get satisfaction from using their strengths and will be attracted to strengths-based organization, Millennials[10] in particular. People often leave organizations where they feel their talents are not being used or developed.
3. Improve individual performance. A strengths focus is likely to improve performance more quickly than a pre-occupation with remedying weaknesses.
4. Build employee engagement. Use of strengths is a key contributor to employee engagement.

174

5. Develop flexibility. When people are selected and deployed on the basis of their strengths there is an increased focus on what can be done rather than what has been done.
6. Improve teamwork. Focusing on strengths within teams creates greater role flexibility, cooperation and positive emotions.
7. Increase diversity and positive inclusion. Understanding strengths encourages the appreciation of difference and diversity. Diverse teams tend to be more creative and perform better.
8. Increase openness to change and the ability to deal with change. The use of strengths generates positive emotions as we saw when we discussed Flow in Chapter 5. People become more open to new experience, less resistant to change, and it contributes to resilience in the face of adversity.
9. Deal more positively with redundancy. Strengths-awareness can help people facing redundancy that they have more to offer and an understanding of where they are likely to be at their best.
10. Contribute to the happiness and fulfillment of employees. Using natural strengths helps people achieve their goals, energizes them, and contributes to a sense of well-being and we know from extensive research the strong positive relationship between employee well-being and many measure of organizational effectiveness.

In a nut-shell, managing employees through awareness and harnessing of strengths, helps people become the best they can be in an environment they believe in. If people know and understand their own strengths and use them positively they are likely to relate to and manage others in a positive way. The positive management of people using strengths as a key theme is a potential source of competitive advantage that is less likely to burn people out and has the potential to increase personal resilience for the long-term.

Recruiting and selecting people through strengths can give competitive advantage in the so-called war for talent and can help organizations thrive in increasingly diverse and changing economic and social conditions not least of which is the need for generational representation in the workforce. The challenge for many employers today is how to satisfy the needs and expectations of different generations in the workforce. For the first time in history there are five generations represented in the workforce.[11] Recruiting and developing people on the basis of their strengths could be part of the answer. It should be noted that we are talking here about strengths in general, and not specifically about personal resilience strengths.

In Chapter 5 we described three of the main strengths questionnaires:

- the VIA Strengths Survey which focuses on your character strengths as a human being;
- StrengthsFinder the widely used measure of personal strengths based on massive data-collection by the Gallup Organization; and
- Realise2 developed and published by the Centre for Applied Positive Psychology in the UK.

The strengths approach has been used in recruitment, induction, team-building, personal development, career planning, project management, and managing change. For a strategic approach to strengths management in organizations see Stavros and Wooten.[12] They use the acronym SOARS to refer to Strengths, Opportunities, Aspirations and Results and align their approach with Appreciative Inquiry.

LEADERSHIP MODELS LIKELY TO ENCOURAGE WELL-BEING AND RESILIENCE

Here we describe a number of broader leadership models that, in our view, proactively promote and sustain resilience, because of their motivational focus and foundation in core human values that are intrinsically satisfying.

The Leadership Challenge

We begin with the five leadership challenges and ten leadership behaviors identified from extensive research by Jim Kouzes and Barry Posner in *The Leadership Challenge*.[13] This is one of the most influential books about leadership in a rapidly changing, ever more competitive world. The authors aim to de-bunk the myths of leadership, especially the view that it depends on inborn characteristics such as charisma. Their main conclusion is that *leadership is an observable, learnable set of practices*. For the authors, the "leadership challenge" is about how leaders get extraordinary things done in organizations. The five practices common to successful leaders are that they:

1. *Model the way* by setting the example, and showing in their behavior what the leader believes to be important, in other words practicing what the leader preaches.
2. *Inspire a shared vision* by envisioning the future and enlisting the support of others in the pursuit of something they believe in.
3. *Challenge the process* by searching for new opportunities as well as experimenting and taking risks in order to get new products, processes, and services adopted.
4. *Enable others to act* by enlisting the support and assistance of everyone involved by fostering collaboration, teamwork, empowerment and building on strengths of others.
5. *Encourage the heart* on the long and sometimes difficult path to success by recognizing individual contribution and celebrating milestones and accomplishments.

The five practices of successful leaders subdivide into ten behaviors that can be modeled and learned, and the ten behaviors further subdivide to create over sixty specific behaviors measured by the Leadership Practices Inventory which is also a powerful 360-degree feedback tool.[14] This approach to leadership development, which is based on over thirty years of research, is likely to build and sustain resilience because of the strong emphasis on vision, values, intrinsic motivation, and engaging with people as human beings.

Transformational Leadership

A second approach to leadership that is likely to boost and encourage resilience because of its impact on people is Bernard Bass's Transformational Leadership,[15] which has also evolved over many years. According to this model, (i) idealized influence, (ii) inspirational motivation, (iii) individualized consideration and (iv) intellectual stimulation, combine and interact resulting in what Bass calls "intrinsic reward," "self-actualization" and "engagement."

Idealized influence: These are leaders who have high standards of moral and ethical conduct, who are held in high personal regard, and who engender loyalty. They choose to do what is right rather than what is simple or expedient. Their consistency and predictability engenders mutual trust and respect.

Inspirational motivation: These leaders have a strong vision for the future based on values and ideals. They stimulate enthusiasm, build confidence, and inspire others through their actions and their language. They challenge employees to be their very best and that they can perform beyond expectations. Feelings of self-confidence, and self-efficacy are engendered.

Individualized consideration: These leadership behaviors are aimed at recognizing the unique and developmental needs of followers, combined with coaching and consultation. These leaders listen and demonstrate empathy and provide personalized social support.

Intellectual stimulation: These leaders challenge organizational norms, encourage divergent thinking, and push for innovation. Employees are encouraged to think for themselves, to challenge cherished assumptions, and to think about old problems in new ways. This promotes employee growth and personal development.

By combining these four qualities, the transformational leader not only achieves superior performance, but also positive morale and engagement.

Authentic Leadership

The third leadership model that is likely to boost and sustain resilience is Bill George's *Authentic Leadership*.[16] George argues that the core purpose of leadership is getting clarity around passion, behavior, connectedness, consistency, and compassion. He sees leadership behavior as practicing what he calls "Solid Values." He stresses the importance of connected relationships and leading from the heart, and demonstrating self-discipline.

Positive Leadership

Finally, we discuss Positive Leadership developed by Kim Cameron and his colleagues at the University of Michigan within the framework of Positive Psychology. In his book Positive Leadership, Cameron[17] describes four positive leadership principles and associated practices. They are:

- *Fostering a positive work climate*. Practices include compassion and forgiveness, which are defined in some detail such as noticing pain, expressing care and concern, acknowledging hurt, identifying optimistic purpose, letting go of grudges, and legitimizing language that communicates virtuousness.

- *Fostering positive relationships among members.* Practices include modeling positive energy by providing opportunities to serve others, developing and managing positive energy networks in stages, capitalizing on employees' strengths, and managing negative energizers in stages.
- *Fostering positive communication.* Practices include regularly using supportive communication (such as five times as much positive feedback as negative), keeping feedback descriptive, and problem not person-focused, and collecting reflected best-self feedback.[18]
- *Associating work with positive meaning.* Practices include helping workers see the impact of what they do on others, highlighting what is meaningful to individuals and benefits produced by the organization, creating a sense of legacy, focusing on contribution goals and not just self-interest and achievement goals.

Kim Cameron sees positive leadership as emphasizing what elevates individuals and organizations (in addition to what challenges them), what goes right in organizations (in addition to what goes wrong), what is life-giving (in addition to what is problematic or life-depleting), what is experienced as good (in addition to what is objectionable), what is extraordinary (in addition to what is merely effective), and what is inspiring (in addition to what is difficult or arduous). There is a strong alignment between positive leadership as defined by Cameron, and Appreciative Inquiry, strengths-based working, and the liberating benefits of positive emotions, all of which enhance and sustain high levels of resilience both individually and collectively. There is a growing trend in leadership theory that recognizes the core role of values and virtues needed by today's leaders that represents a significant shift away from the model of the lone-wolf leader pre-occupied with wealth, status and power that was so dominant in the eighties and nineties and came crashing down in 2007–8.[19]

STRATEGIC, ORGANIZATION-WIDE INTERVENTIONS

In this section we address more systematic, comprehensive organizational approaches to resilience as a contributor to organizational success. We introduce a number of different stories which we will discuss further in the final chapter of this book.

1. The first story is based on the conviction by top leadership that resilience is what is needed without any prior analysis of need. This was the basis of the US Army's Comprehensive Soldier Fitness Program.
2. In the second story we describe how resilience-building was used as a key element in the transformation of a strategically important manufacturing site.
3. Then we describe how resilience thinking and practices were built into a financial services start-up from the beginning.

A Total Belief in Resilience: The Us Army Comprehensive Soldier Fitness Program

We tell this story in some detail because it represents a major initiative, which despite the military context, has enormous implications for employers in general. The US Army has been at war in Iraq and Afghanistan for over a decade. Soldiers have been rotating between combat and home repeatedly, culminating in unprecedented levels of stress, suicides and broken relationships within families. The Army needed to do something to help its soldiers and their families cope. In harnessing resilience-building based on good psychological research, the US Army adopted a holistic capacity-building approach, rather than merely seeking to ameliorate symptoms of sustained stress.

The Army's Comprehensive Soldier Fitness Program (CSF) is officially described by the US Army Chief of Staff as

> a preventative program that seeks to enhance psychological resilience among all members of the Army community, which includes soldiers, family members, and Department of the Army civilians. CSF is not a medical treatment program. Rather CSF helps those community members who are psychologically healthy face life's adversities—including combat and prolonged separation from loved ones—by providing evidence-based training. (General W. Casey, U.S. Army Chief of Staff)[20]

Martin Seligman, the pioneer of the highly successful Penn Resilience (depression prevention) Program and professor of psychology at

Pennsylvania University, describes in his book *Flourish*,[21] how he was summoned in 2008 to a meeting chaired by General Casey, was introduced to the meeting as a world expert on resilience, and was told that the Army wanted its own resilience program for all 1.2 million soldiers, and also their families and army civilians. Seligman was then introduced to Brigadier General Corum, who was heading up the project, and General Casey asked them both to report back with their proposals in 60 days! The Army clearly knew what it wanted and wanted it fast.

The US Army was formally constituted in 1784 but did not take the physical fitness of all active personnel seriously until 1940 when fitness standards were codified and embedded into Army life for the first time. In 2008 the Army took a similar radical step, this time focusing on psychological fitness, under the banner of resilience, when it committed to providing resilience training, not just as a remedy for Post Traumatic Stress Disorder, but also as a builder of psychological capacity, building on soldiers' strengths to help them stay effective in their various roles throughout their Army careers, and also to provide training according to individual need.

There are four key components to The Comprehensive Soldier Fitness Program:

1. An online survey of psychological fitness called the Global Assessment Tool. It comprises 105 questions takes most people less than 15 minutes to complete, and is to be taken bi-annually by all soldiers of all ranks. The GAT provides confidential assessments of emotional fitness, social fitness, family fitness, and spiritual fitness. There are separate versions of the test for families and Department of the Army civilians. The test provides immediate confidential feedback on areas of strength and also refers soldiers, families and civilians to elective online courses in areas of need. By September 2010, over 800,000 soldiers had taken the assessment. It will become the world's largest database of psychological information that can be tracked over time for evaluation studies and also for research on a scale that has hitherto not been possible.
2. Online training was specifically developed with modules on Emotional Fitness, Family Fitness, Social Fitness, and Spiritual Fitness all developed by eminent positive psychologists. The modules are elective and soldiers can take basic and more advanced versions as needed. In addition, a fifth module on Post Traumatic

Growth is mandatory. The aim here is to teach soldiers the conditions under which growth is most likely to happen in response to trauma.
3. Mandatory resilience training at every Army leader development school was introduced.
4. The US Army Master Resilience Training (MRT) is a ten-day program of study run by the University of Pennsylvania and other Army units that teaches resilience skills to non-commissioned officers who then teach these skills to others. The skills enhance handling adversity, help prevent depression and PTSD, but equally are designed to enhance overall well-being and performance.

Master Resilience Trainers are the core of the Army's resilience-training program. We will describe it in a little more detail. The first eight days of MRT teaches the skills elements derived from the Penn Resiliency Program using a combination of formal inputs and discussions in plenary sessions, and smaller breakout sessions where participants are taught to apply and practice what they have learned. During the last three days of the preparation phase the sergeants are taught how to teach the resilience skills they have learned to other soldiers. Day Nine, called Sustainment, focuses on reinforcing resilience skills over the course of a military career and applying them in the Military context. Day Ten, called Enhancement, teaches techniques originally developed in sports psychology and covers mental skills, confidence building, goal setting, energy management, and imagery. Days Nine and Ten were developed by Army personnel.

The five-day preparation phase of MRT has five Modules[22]

1. *Module 1: Resilience* (one and a half days) covers the underlying principles of resilience and clarifies common misunderstandings. This module focuses on the six core competencies that are used to build resilience:
   a. Self-awareness of the thoughts, emotions and behavior patterns that are counter-productive
   b. Self-regulation of impulses, thinking, emotions, and behaviors to achieve goals, and the willingness and ability to express emotion
   c. Mental agility, thinking flexibly and accurately
   d. Character Strengths, identifying them and using them to overcome challenges and difficulties

    e. Connection, building strong relationships by appropriate communication, empathy and helping behaviors.
2. *Module 2: Building Mental Toughness* (one and a half days) covers the skills that build mental toughness and effective problem solving. Specifically, the skills taught are:
    a. ABC thinking is the ability to recognize that our emotional reactions to events are strongly influenced by our beliefs about the events. Changing our beliefs helps change our automatic emotional response from unrealistically negative to realistically positive. The exercises focus on both professional and personal examples.
    b. Explanatory styles and thinking traps (e.g. jumping to conclusions, black and white thinking) either heighten or hinder performance. Understanding the negative ones helps to limit their harmful consequences.
    c. Icebergs (or deeply held beliefs such as "I can deal with anything that comes my way" or "Deep down I am a loser") can have profound unconscious effects on performance both positively and negatively. Icebergs can be surfaced and challenged using simple techniques.
    d. Energy management focuses on techniques such as meditation, controlled breathing, progressive muscle relaxation, and rejuvenation strategies such as prayer, exercise, sleep, and laughter.
    e. Problem solving using a six-step model to accurately identify contributing causes and identify solution strategies and strategies for avoiding confirmation bias.
    f. Minimizing catastrophic thinking which is defined as ruminating about irrational worst-case thinking and replacing it with effective contingency planning.
    g. Cultivating gratitude, which is called "Hunt the Good Stuff," is based on keeping a three blessings journal that is routinely shared among MRT participants.
3. *Model 3: Identifying Character Strengths* (one day) covers identifying individual and team strengths and practice using top strengths to overcome challenges and difficulties to reach a goal. Sergeants complete VIA (described in Chapter 5) and identify individual strengths and any patterns that might exist in the group. After discussing individual strengths the MRT participants practice identifying strengths in others and how to use available strengths to complete a mission. The focus is not just on the use of strengths as

leaders but also in their families and how working with strengths can build stronger connections between soldiers in a unit and also within their families.

4. *Module 4: Strengthening Relationships* (one day) covers techniques and skills for building strong constructive relationships. Three skills are covered;
   a. Active-constructive responding
   b. Effective process-based, as opposed to person-based, feedback
   c. Assertive communication and how to avoid passive and aggressive communication style.

5. *Module 5 Consolidation of learning (half a day)* identifies key themes and completion of an individual resilience development plan.

The first official MRT course was conducted in November 2009. Each certified MRT instructor works with his or her unit leadership to identify and schedule dedicated blocks of training time on a regular basis to cover all soldiers. All active component units are required to conduct two hours of resilience training, per quarter. The MRT trainers are able to independently teach 12 units ranging in length from 30 minutes to two hours covering all the subjects they learned in the five modules of the MRT course.

In addition to formally teaching others, MRT trainers are expected to live the skills they have been taught, and use them during formal and informal counseling. MRTs also act as their Commander's advisor regarding total fitness and resilience training related issues. They also identify when to refer soldiers for professional counseling to behavioral health providers, chaplains or other appropriate resources. By January 2013, the Army had 14,296 Certified Master Resilience Trainers, and over a million soldiers had received resilience training. The US Army committed to introducing Resilience Training for all Commissioned and Non-Commissioned Officers by the end of 2011.

In December 2011 the results of a 15-month evaluation of the impact of MRT on GAT scores were released.[23] The study evaluated GAT scores of eight randomly selected brigade combat teams, four of which had received MRT, and four had not. The GAT scores of the combat teams receiving the resilience training were significantly higher than the others, irrespective of other variables, such as leadership and cohesion. Even with severe budgetary constraints, the official view is that resilience training, like physical training, will be a permanent feature of Army operations because it helps soldiers, their families, and department civilians thrive under demanding and difficult conditions, while at the same time minimizing sickness and stress.

We discuss the implications and lessons for employers of this massive intervention in the next chapter but first the story of how resilience was a key driver in a major culture transformation of a critically important manufacturing site.

Resilience as a Driver of Change: Using Resilience-Building as a Key Component in the Transformation of a Strategically Important but Underperforming Manufacturing Site

The site in this example produced billions of dollars worth of product annually, but it was not a happy site. While production targets were aggressively being raised and met, a series of cost-cutting exercises had been put in place with large-scale reduction in the number of people on the site to help make the site globally competitive in terms of costs and quality. The rapid series of re-organizations and associated RIFs had come as a shock to the site as it had been, and seen itself as, a flag-ship organization that for many years had been stable, confident and assured.

The pace of change was increasing and the pressure from the company to produce more and more, with fewer and fewer people, seemed relentless. Mistakes were beginning to happen, internal and external audits were drawing attention to lapses in standards, and quality assurance issues were increasing in frequency. Problems with good manufacturing practice, housekeeping, and human errors were increasing.

Above all, employee engagement, as measured by internal audits, hit an all-time low. Previous general managers of the site had heroically maintained production and delivered product but the workforce had become weary, worried and cynical. They were burning out.

The new GM had inherited a critically important site that was beset with problems on a whole range of issues from morale, quality and consistency to breaks in production. She was under pressure from her corporate masters to solve the problems and to deliver consistent quality as quickly as possible. The middle managers were being singled out for blame, as it was felt they needed to accept the new

185

order and deliver what was expected. If the problems could not be resolved rapidly the site would have to close and production moved elsewhere, possibly overseas.

The new GM took over the management of a site leadership team that was struggling and felt under constant pressure, and individual members were wondering how much longer they could cope. There was, as she put it, "a huge lack of trust" within the leadership team itself and across the site. The leadership team members felt stressed and unsupported. They did not act as a united management team. She realized that the culture needed to be changed to one that was based, not on blame and threats, but on engagement and well-being.

She knew she had to start at the top. Without a united team that was dealing positively with the pressures, rather than succumbing to them, she knew she could not transform the middle managers and eventually the site as a whole. She decided to bring about a culture-change based on building resilience and well-being rather than fear and threats. She believed that a focus on resilience would deepen her team's self-understanding as individuals, help them understand their stress-points, enable them to cope positively with the sustained pressure, and increase their confidence. This, in turn, would allow them to be open and trusting with each other, which would lead to a change in the way they managed and supported their own direct reports. In short, she saw resilience as a tool to help them manage pressure positively, instead of endless fire-fighting and blaming others. A cohesive, positive management team was the first step towards transforming the site.

The first change that her leadership team, and other people on the site, experienced was her style. She actively showed appreciation, she asked many questions, and listened well. She showed concern for everyone's welfare and well-being, at all levels of the organization. She was always polite and considerate, even in the face of set-backs and problems. She made it clear that she would not tolerate incivility and rudeness, which had become an entrenched habit around the site. She made it clear what she valued and showed it in her behavior. She was role-modeling her values. Inevitably, some initially saw this as a sign of weakness, while others were skeptical, believing that her style was just a front to disarm people and that it would disappear under pressure.

The next thing the new GM did, within two months of arriving at the site, was to initiate a leadership team transformation process with a combined focus on team dynamics, personal growth and individual resilience. The first phase consisted of three two-day offsites, addressing such issues as how to become a high performing team, creating a new mission and vision that reflected current realities, understanding and constructively addressing problems. Half of the first two-day workshop was devoted to the individual resilience-building that was a core theme throughout the transformation process. In addition, all the members of the leadership team completed online assessments, including *Leadership Impact* and *i-resilience* and other measures of personality and resilience.

Each member of the team then had a personal and confidential personal development discussion with an external consultant, and agreed their development objectives, which if they wished could focus on personal resilience issues. Two-thirds of the team agreed, for at least one of their development objectives, to improve some aspect of individual resilience—ranging from personal confidence, assertive communication and managing pessimism to emotional control in the face of setbacks. Having agreed the objectives the external consultant provided regular one-on-one coaching between the offsites to members of the team. Periodically, the team would jointly review how they were feeling about their personal and team progress including building their individual resilience.

Another feature of the transformation process was to introduce the idea of a strengths-based organization. Emphasizing and building on the positive became a theme, though there were times when the urgency and the unexpected criticality of an issue warranted more directive and uncompromising action from the GM. Although this was sometimes seen as a setback, and a gift to the skeptics, a bedrock of goodwill and understanding had been established across the site, that was not there previously, and the negative reaction from the site was not so strong. Progress might have been temporarily slowed but was not reversed. A scaled-down but similar process was initiated for all the people managers on the site, and a change agent program was also initiated.

The site continued to experience problems both in terms of quality and other issues, but the leadership team was now united under a common vision, and holding each other to behavioral standards. This in turn set a good example to the rest of the site, which has become more flexible, adaptable and confident to deal effectively with the unpredictable and pressurized environment that they accept as normal.

Within twelve months, the site's employee engagement score increased dramatically, manufacturing targets were being exceeded, internal and external audits were being passed, and the site was meeting safety, housekeeping, and quality targets. The GM commented:

> When I came to this site, the leadership team and the site as a whole was caught in a downward spiral. There was pressure from above to close the site and move production elsewhere. My job was to fix it or close it down. By focusing on individual resilience the leadership team gained strength and the capability to face the issues, rescue themselves from a downward spiral of blame and negativity, and to turn around a disengaged workforce to become actively involved in addressing problems and building a more secure future. Without the focus on individual resilience and strengths-based leadership the change in the leadership team and the site could not have happened so quickly.

Building Resilience into the Culture of a Financial Services Start-Up

Starting a new business can be stressful and demanding. There is much at stake, the pressure to move quickly is immense, the risk of failure is high, working hours are long and hard, and the support and disciplines associated with more established companies is frequently lacking. Fast-moving, chaotic and agile are the hall-marks of early-stage start-ups. For some it is a thrill while for others it is a considerable strain, often with no-one to talk to or with the time and inclination to listen. Burnout and sometimes suicides grab the headlines. It is part and parcel of the entrepreneurial endeavor. Venture capitalists take very seriously the business proposition, the marketing plans, and the financial strategy. They often seek to ensure there is a competent management team in place for start-ups in which they seek to invest, but they rarely if ever assess the capacity of the key individuals to thrive under the pressurized conditions.

One entrepreneur who was launching his own private equity business, having previously been part of a larger company, decided he was going to build resilience into the culture of his organization from the outset. Within a week of starting, he introduced the entire staff of twenty to the benefits of managing and sustaining individual resilience as part of a team event in which they jointly created a mission and a vision for the new business.

They jointly defined the new firm's culture as:

- happy, productive employees;
- collegial, open culture supporting an integrated life;
- career advancement opportunities;
- leadership in place to manage growth.

In referring to "integrated life," they were focusing attention on the various components that contributed to well-being and resilience, instead of the pursuit of work-life balance. They decided to focus collectively on physical activity, sleep and diet. An early initiative was to supply all employees with an electronic device the size of a USB stick, with mobile devices and access to a website that compiled information about the individual's activity, physical health, sleep, and diet onto charts. Most of the information was inputted automatically using Wi-Fi from the device or from smartphones phones or i-pads, and the rest was entered manually on the website. The MD said it had changed his life, as he was simultaneously monitoring and adjusting his physical activity, his sleep, and his diet, which at times could be difficult as his job involved a lot of international travel. He said all of the employees felt the focus on resilience during a demanding and potentially stressful phase of the company's early growth had not only helped them cope but also enjoy themselves. The fact that each individual's progress could be shown as a comparison with all other employees, fired up the more highly competitive employees, though others decided not to display their personal rankings.

Resilience was on the agenda as a core strength of the new business from the outset, and was regularly discussed and reviewed at the biannual offsite events, usually lasting two or three days. The next phase was to collectively address strengths, and review and build positive emotions. The focus on resilience as a strength of the new business was as popular with the more junior staff, as it was with the partners.

In the next chapter we discuss the different and powerful ways that a focus on resilience can play in underpinning, facilitating or supporting organizational change or sustaining performance in challenging or difficult times.

PART 3

THE FUTURE OF RESILIENCE AND ITS ROLE IN ACHIEVING WIDER ORGANIZATIONAL OBJECTIVES

CHAPTER 8

RESILIENCE-BUILDING: IMPLICATIONS FOR EMPLOYERS

In this chapter we provide an overview of resilience-building that emerges from the discussion in earlier chapters. We go on to pull together the practical implications by sketching out eight scenarios for using or building individual resilience in the workplace.

WHAT HAVE WE SOUGHT TO EMPHASIZE ABOUT INDIVIDUAL RESILIENCE?

The common view of resilience as a specific capacity to bounce back or recover from setbacks, disappointment, or extreme events is rather narrow and does not do justice to the complex, multi-dimensional nature of this important aspect of our lives. Once resilience is recognized as both the process and outcome of keeping going and staying effective in the face of threat, challenge, and adversity, the developmental implications and possibilities become clearer. The abiding message of this book is that individual resilience, as strength or capacity, can be improved by a variety of developmental interventions and techniques.

Our feelings of how resilient we are can vary from day to day, but the resilience of our response to events is underpinned by a consistent set of personal characteristics, abilities, and attitudes. Drawing on our review of the research, we have clustered these into four main components: *Confidence, Social Support, Adaptability* and *Purposefulness*. Central to these components are well recognized resilience factors such as self-belief, sense of purpose, and problem-solving ability. However, we have argued that a full assessment and understanding of an individual's resilience starting point requires a broader, more holistic view of the enduring characteristics that he or she brings into any situation, including the workplace. As a framework for providing this view we use the Five-Factor Model of personality, supplemented by various measures of attitudes and abilities that have particular relevance for resilience. These underlying personal characteristics interact with our experiences in different situations, producing fluctuations in how we see our resilience from day to day. Fluctuations in mood, as well as situational influences such as pressure to conform or obedience to authority, will influence the manifestation of resilience in one's behavior on a day by day basis, or from one situation to another.

Situational influences, and the way we respond to them, also produce longer-term changes that boost or undermine our capacity for coping with circumstances in a resilient way. For those interested in building resilience in an organizational context it is, therefore, important to understand the main sources of workplace pressure and support. To facilitate assessment and understanding of these situational factors, we have used the six-factor ASSET framework. In this way we have provided a framework for understanding the individual and another for understanding the work situation, so that it is easier to analyze the way resilience can be built (or undermined) through the interaction between the employee and his or her work situation.

HOW COMMON IS RESILIENCE?

In this book we have focused primarily on the broader, more holistic concept of resilience. One way of seeing this is to think about heroic, as opposed to routine, resilience. Heroic resilience, such as surviving being lost in the jungle for months with only snakes and insects for food, is a capacity seen in only a minority of the population. By contrast, routine resilience is a quality that can be seen to some degree in almost all people. This routine resilience is increasingly recognized as being quite normal and widespread. Martin Seligman has pointed out that the development of a broadly optimistic outlook probably had survival value for our species in evolutionary terms (optimism being one of the key drivers of personal resilience). Today, most people in individualistic western societies are broadly optimistic. This is not always the case in collectivist Asian cultures, where people may be more likely to draw on social support than on personal optimism.[1] It is important to remember that, in addition to its physical/biological foundations, resilience has its foundations in our emotional life, our social life, and relationships, our values and beliefs, our goals, and our mental and cognitive habits, and even a genetic component, as we discussed in Chapters 1 and 4.

OBSERVATIONS ON DEVELOPING RESILIENCE

So what are the implications of recognizing that resilience can be strengthened through learning and development? An individual's resilience might be lower than normal because of severe and sustained pressure at work, worries about job security, problems at home, or simply not sleeping well. Alternatively, an individual may have always had a tendency to rumination, self-blame, and harsh self-criticism. One individual might often feel gloomy, with work relationships that are frequently strained. Another individual might begin to panic when under pressure and make decisions that put undue pressure on direct reports. Working long hours that never ease up, constant 24/7 email, travel, and long periods away from home and family all combine to put sustained pressure on individual employees. In all these circumstances, resilience-building can make a difference to being effective in the present and stronger in the future.

Related to the general point that resilience can be learned is the clear conclusion that one size does not fit all. It is not possible to identify the six or ten steps to increased resilience or the essential components that would work for all people in all situations. Training interventions can be based on a general offering from which individuals make their own assessment and identify what is going to work best for them. This was the approach adopted by the US Army and the strategically important manufacturing site fighting for survival that we described in the previous chapter. Alternatively, training can be provided that reflects the findings of a systematic data-gathering exercise, but even here individuals will choose what to focus on and what works best for them. Either way, there is no generic prescription that will work equally well for all people. The US Army's mandatory element of the Comprehensive Soldier Fitness Program focused on self-awareness, self-control, mental agility, character strengths, and building stronger relationships. Even with this standardized approach, individual soldiers will take different lessons out of the resilience offering. In Appendix III, we provide a comprehensive list of subjects that can be covered in resilience training and development that can be drawn upon to customize interventions to meet specific needs and requirements. Not all topics will be equally relevant, and more or less emphasis can be placed on individual elements in different contexts.

The key thing to remember here is that training alone, however good, will not bring about sustainable and lasting changes in resilience. There must be opportunity, encouragement, and support for experimentation and behavior change over protracted periods. There must be clear support from people in leadership roles, who also act in accordance with the principles that are being espoused. In effect, the best way to capitalize on the investment of resources in resilience training and development is to make it a critical part of a culture change strategy over a period of time measured in years rather than months. That is not to say however that there will not be measurable benefits within months as indeed the US Army found.

LESSONS FROM THE US ARMY RESILIENCE PROGRAM

The US Army Comprehensive Soldier Fitness Program,[2] which despite its name embraces families and Army civilians, is a strategic culture change initiative designed to make resilience (or psychological fitness) as fundamental and normal to Army life as is physical fitness. It is the world's largest and most comprehensive organizational intervention on resilience, which is being subjected to continuous evaluation and improvement. As such, it offers many lessons for employing organizations of all kinds. There are ten clear lessons.

What Corporations can Learn from the Comprehensive Soldier Fitness Program[3]

1. The importance of total and unequivocal commitment from the top of the organization. General Casey stated in January 2011 that Implementing Comprehensive Soldier Fitness was one of his top priorities, with full support from Congress and Department of the Army and a budget to match.[4]

2. The comprehensive nature of the Program is unprecedented, as it reaches all soldiers, commissioned and non-commissioned officers, their families, and Department of the Army Civilians.

3. The vision of the CSF is to create an Army that is just as psychologically fit, as it is physically fit. The focus is on a vision that psychological resilience will become just as ingrained in the culture and ethos of the Amy as physical fitness has since 1940. Resilience-building will no longer be seen as a sign of weakness but as a significant contributor to the Army's effectiveness in the 21st century.

4. Related to the vision, the CSF Program is seen as a significant culture change for the Army, embracing a holistic approach (physical, emotional, spiritual, social, and family), regular systematic confidential assessments, mandatory leadership training, elective individualized on-line training modules, flexible resilience skills training for all soldiers, constant evaluation of impact, and a commitment to continuous improvement.

5. The focus is not just a moment in time as a reaction to a looming crisis. The Army adopted a proactive capacity-building approach. It was clearly recognized that resilience is not built by attending a lecture or a course. The Army took a long-term strategic view of the benefits of higher levels of resilience.

6. A distinctive feature of the CSF program is that it seeks to build resilience over the entire Army career with its different stages, as well as the combat deployment cycle. In corporate terms, this has implications for recruitment, onboarding, transition into people management, leadership development, support for employees who travel a great deal, or are dealing with stressful change such as mergers, acquisitions, RIFs, etc.

7. Responsibility for the Program was located in Army Operations and, significantly, not in Medical. This in itself sends a message. Maybe, a corporate resilience program should not be located within the HR or Learning and Development function.

8. Apart from components that are specific to the Army, such as the Global Assessment Tool, and days nine and ten of the Master Resilience Training, almost all the material on which it is based is in the public domain, either as academic published papers or books by the relevant academic researchers that were brought together by Martin Seligman, and that the Army used to design various components of the Program. With suitable acknowledgements and appropriate permissions, any corporation could design

its own variation of a culture-changing resilience program, suitably adapted and scaled to its own needs. The reason the Army was able to move so quickly was that it asked for only evidence-based and proven methods to be incorporated into the Program. There was little innovation and no experimenting. Hence, pilot-studies were not deemed necessary, though the Army is embarked on a program of systematic and regular evaluations of impact.

9. Corporations could decide to adopt an evidence-based approach in response to a current need, or they could undertake a systematic audit such as the ASSET well-being survey and plan accordingly. The Army recognized that the need to address and build resilience across the organization was urgent, and they adopted a direct intervention that was both strategic and culture changing. Some corporations that are facing a crisis or symptoms of sustained pressure or severe stress can adopt an approach similar to that of the US Army while others may choose the get the data first and plan accordingly. Both approaches will work. It all depends on the sense of urgency.

10. The US Army introduced group intelligence testing to the world in the First World War, and also critical incident analysis in the Second World War (and the British Army, incidentally, invented what became known as assessment centers).[5] It looks as though the US Army is showcasing an evidence-based, culture-changing, comprehensive approach to resilience-building as a source of competitive advantage from which many corporations could learn and adapt to their needs.

PRACTICAL SCENARIOS FOR RESILIENCE-BUILDING INTERVENTIONS IN ORGANIZATIONS

We have identified eight scenarios for increasing individual resilience to help improve organizational performance as well as the well-being and engagement of employees.

Resilience development as:

1. general performance enhancer;
2. remedy or response to stress or unusual circumstances;
3. accelerator of team development and/or integration;

4. enabler for the transformation of an underperforming organization;
5. core capability in organizations that routinely face demanding and stressful conditions;
6. core culture builder in start-ups;
7. essential component of leadership development, especially in difficult and challenging times that is the norm today;
8. supporting organizational transformation and culture change.

We describe these scenarios in more detail below as separate and different contexts though in reality they will often overlap.

Resilience-Building as a General Performance Enhancer

In this scenario, employers help individual employees review and build personal resilience as a capacity-building process in the present and for the future. The underlying assumption here is that almost all employees can benefit from raising their average resilience levels. The employer is not in crisis and despite a challenging environment is not suffering from problems caused by sustained pressure leading to stress. Current business goals are being met, but there is a recognition that a great deal is being expected of employees.

Offering elective workshops, typically one or two days in length, is a recognition that times are tough and that we can all benefit from assessing and building levels of individual resilience. It would be important to position the workshops as building on strengths and not as a remedial response to presumed weakness. The workshops can also be offered to work teams and management teams, with a focus on discussing how the benefits at the individual level can be supported and harnessed within the team. In addition, coaching on resilience can also be offered.

Some groups, such as sales teams and project teams delivering against tight deadlines, feel that they are under constant pressure, and have found individual resilience-building helpful in staying on top of the pressures.

Resilience-building would be one topic among many that the organization offers to help employees be more effective in current and future roles. We have consistently found that such workshops are popular at all levels in an organization because they give the individual time to slow down and reflect not only on their jobs but their lives as a whole. In addition it builds confidence that there are tried and tested techniques and tools that they can use to help them be effective in challenging or difficult circumstances and stronger in the future.

Resilience-Building as a Remedy or Response to Stress or Unusual Circumstances

In this scenario, the organization has suffered a major set-back or crisis. The employees are worried, and are under enormous pressure to put things right quickly.

Individual resilience-building through workshops and coaching can be offered on an elective basis, to show recognition of how employees are feeling but also to offer techniques and help that enable employees to stay focused and deliver the changes and results needed while the company is in, or recovering from, a crisis. As we described earlier, the company started on a small scale providing voluntary workshops on individual resilience-building, and progressed to incorporating it into senior executive development programs. Individual resilience-building can help an organization work through a crisis and become part of the culture.

Resilience-Building to Accelerate Team Development and/or Integration

Individual resilience-building can be built into a team development/ integration process. In one case the divisional manager in a large bank was trying to bring together the business heads of subsidiary companies and functions that had not worked together before as a team. As a result of the economic collapse in 2008, the parent company was facing a crisis on a scale that it had never experienced before in its 160-year history.

A senior executive in a manufacturing company was trying to integrate the leadership teams of two very disparate sites belonging to two separate companies within the Group, one green-field, latest technology and un-unionized, the result of an acquisition, and the other forty years old, established technology, long standing leadership team, and highly unionized. In both cases there was a high level of suspicion mingled with fear, a feeling of being harshly judged or evaluated by new and unfamiliar standards that they were being asked to sign up to, culminating in a high level of defensiveness and a desire to defend the past which was very different in both sites.

The two senior executives, one in financial services and the other in manufacturing, introduced individual resilience-building into the team development/integration process. In the manufacturing company the two site teams came together to create a shared vision and to explore how individual resilience could help them in the transition process to an integrated operation. In the financial services organization, the heads of the various business and functions came together for the first time and individual resilience was a key theme in breaking down barriers.

In both cases, the personal discussions about resilience and how it can help both at work and in one's private life, together with experiencing tools that build resilience, led to an openness and personal disclosure that is uncommon within groups in transition where fear and defensiveness prevail. The recognition that the members of the new combined team were all human beings struggling with stress, pressure, fears, and anxiety, led to a unifying feeling that was strengthened by jointly experiencing the tools and exercises that are designed to build resilience. The response was not cynical. In fact it was the opposite, engendering enthusiasm, compassion, and understanding. Martin Seligman reported a similar finding among the platoon and drill sergeants (almost universally tough and demanding characters) who underwent the Master Resilience Training in the US Army. They rated the training amongst the best they had ever received. [6]

Resilience-Building as an Enabler to Help Turn Round an Underperforming Organization

To be part of an under-performing team or organization can be stressful enough, especially when job security is at risk, or the business is threatened with complete failure or closure. It is even more stressful for people in a leadership role who are responsible for improving performance overall. Sustained pressure can cause stress symptoms that undermine health, energy, and personal effectiveness. It can become a dangerous spiral if not caught early enough. Introducing resilience-building to these individuals, whether in the form of workshops or one-on-one coaching, or both, can have a significant impact on individual performance leading to increased capacity to manage change positively.

The emphasis is on building on personal strengths, finding where energy is released rather than consumed, and finding alternative behaviors, and habits of thought, words, and feelings that help the individual remain, or become, more effective, during a difficult and challenging transition. It is often said that uncertainty is the new certainty, and change is the new constant. Whereas this is true a lot of the time, the rate and scale of change will vary from high to very high. During a period of transition, when the very survival of the site or business is at stake, providing resilience-building support can take some of the pressure off, increase confidence to cope, and help create more cohesiveness within a leadership team. When the rate and scale of change moves from very high back to a more normal high, the managers have acquired a sustained level of resilience such that the need for coaching and/or training may no longer be necessary.

Using Resilience-Building to Build a Stronger, More Capable Organization that Routinely Faces Demanding and Stressful Conditions

Probably the most common scenario for an organization-wide resilience development program is where higher than average levels of stress are experienced because of the nature and purpose of the organization. This would apply in particular to police forces, fire and rescue, armed services, and health care and social services, and possibly many public-facing roles. As we saw earlier the US Army's resilience-based Comprehensive Soldier Fitness Program is designed not only to help soldiers and their families cope with the pressures of Army life, but also to strengthen the overall capability of all army personnel to thrive and be effective. The benefit to these organizations, which live daily with exceptional stress levels, of the resilience intervention is the increased effectiveness and well-being of all personnel, to help them do difficult and demanding jobs.

Resilience-Building for Start-Ups

Any business start-up can be a stressful time. There is so much to do, a feeling of too little time, and often a team of people who have not worked together, and do not know each other well. Personalities substitute for effective leadership behavior; people become anxious and worried after initial enthusiasm and aspiration need to be converted into business results. Similar pressures occur when venture capitalists invest in small businesses, or when a team is put together specifically for a critical product development or launch on which the hopes of the company are resting.

In all these cases introducing individual resilience development and/or coaching would make a significant difference. It would not on its own secure successful outcomes, but would help individual team members not only cope positively with the pressures, setbacks and disappointment along the way, but more importantly would help each individual function at his or her best, despite the pressures. We saw in earlier how resilience-building was incorporated into the start-up team's development for all employees including the partners of a newly formed specialized asset-management business.

Resilience-Building as a Key Part of Leadership Development

Following a meeting at which the business benefits of resilience-building were discussed, and the US Army program was described, the global head of HR for a fast-food company employing over several hundred thousand people around the world, declared that resilience was going to be one of his 10 leadership messages that he would always communicate to all functions and business units around the world.

We also described in the previous chapter how a company incorporated resilience development into an executive development program that it ran in collaboration with Harvard Business School. The US Army has incorporated resilience into all officer training as part of its longer term culture change strategy to make resilience (psychological fitness) as critical to its effectiveness as physical fitness has been for the last seventy years.

Resilience as a Driver of Organizational Transformation

We saw in the previous chapter how resilience assessment, training and coaching were incorporated into a transformation process of a threatened but strategically important manufacturing site. The focus on resilience helped build confidence and increased effectiveness of individuals within the leadership team during a bumpy ride over a twelve month period that saw the site not only escape the threat of closure but begin to emerge as a place of new investment and very high employee engagement scores.

The General Manager concluded that the transformation probably could have been achieved without the focus on individual resilience, but it would have been more painful and would have taken a lot longer, and time was in short supply.

THE FUTURE OF RESILIENCE IN ORGANIZATIONAL LIFE

In a very short period (possibly around twenty years), resilience-building has shifted from a narrow focus as a remedial or preventative measure designed to overcome stress and anxiety (as with the Penn Resilience Program and early training interventions with stressful sales roles), to a broader focus as capacity or strength-builder to enable people, teams and organizations to sustain high levels of performance in challenging and difficult circumstances. It has also shifted from a focus primarily on cognitive functioning (e.g. understanding and attacking automatic negative thoughts), to a broader construct embracing the whole life of the individual where personal strengths are identified and built upon in the broader context of positive emotions, social relationships, and meaning, as well as the physical dimension. We see this as a whole person approach to resilience, as distinct from cognitive/emotional skills approach.

We foresee an increased focus on building and sustaining individual resilience as a key element in transformation and change processes within organizations of all kinds, especially where time pressures and the stakes are very high. We also foresee an increased focus on resilience in organizations generally to help equip people in all roles to manage effectively.

Based on our observation and our recent experience, it is our considered view that resilience will increasingly be incorporated into leadership and executive development programs. Alongside the growing emphasis on personal integrity and authenticity, and the growing recognition of the role of character strengths and key positive emotions for those in leadership roles such as gratitude and compassion, there will be growing recognition that leaders need to build and protect their resilience in order to stay effective in today's challenging and pressurized working environment. In this way, they not only stay effective and strong to challenge as well as support others, they become less vulnerable to making organizationally poor or ethically bad decisions when under pressure or feeling high levels of stress.

We have presented a framework that encompasses the very individual nature of each person's resilience on the one hand, and the main sources of workplace pressure and support that are present in any organizational context, on the other. This is a new way of looking at the development of personal resilience in the work context, and is designed to facilitate a holistic, strategic and organization-wide approach to boosting resilience and success for all. We hope that our readers find it as useful as we have in supporting our clients in recent years.

There can clearly be no doubt that, by building and protecting the resilience of the workforce, employers not only contribute to the overall success of their organizations, but also boost the well-being and engagement of organization members.

APPENDIX I

A SHORT GUIDE TO USING THIS BOOK

A short guide to using this book in designing your own resilience-building interventions.

Overview of chapters	Specific relevance for design
Chapter 1 ■ Addresses the question of individual differences and sets out a framework for understanding personal resilience strengths and risks. Includes a more detailed definition of resilience, as well as a review of the relevant research and information on a variety of diagnostic tools and approaches.	■ Provides a research-based foundation for understanding and explaining the nature of personal resilience and how it develops. ■ Sets out a four-component model that can be used to describe and evaluate an individual's resilience resources. ■ Introduces some of the main resilience diagnostic measures to incorporate into the self-assessment/development planning element of your intervention.

Chapter 2

- Looks at the individual in the workplace context. Describes the main sources of workplace pressure and support and how these are likely to affect each of us differently. Focuses on the interaction between a person and his or her work situation, and the way in which an individual's resilience resources may be boosted or undermined by this interaction.

  - Provides a research-based foundation for understanding and explaining the different sources of workplace pressure and support.
  - Explains how the process of resilience development works on the job.
  - Sets out a six-component framework that can be used to assess and manage the impact of workplace factors on personal resilience.

Chapter 3

- Tells the story "from then to now", for those who have a professional interest in understanding the background to where we are today, who want to take a broad, systemic approach and to make sure resilience development is not just a passing fad in their organization.

  - Provides a broad, historical perspective to help with design and buy-in for new programs
  - Explains how resilience development fits with organizational stress management and employee well-being programs
  - Describes in more detail how knowledge about workplace pressure and leadership impact has been brought together to improve well-being and resilience.

Chapters 4 and 5

- Looks at what individuals can do to build their resilience, both on their own and with the support of their employers. The emphasis here is on resilience-building as a personal quest and a "whole-life" endeavor – even if the catalyst and support are provided by the work context.

  - Provide detailed information and further reading on techniques that can be learned and applied by individuals within or outside the context of organizational resilience-building courses and programs:
    i. The two most influential and broadly applicable resilience development techniques
    ii. Techniques that are particularly well suited to boosting each of the four main components of resilience (Confidence etc.)

Continued

Continued

Overview of chapters	Specific relevance for design

Chapters 6 and 7
■ Focus on approaches that managers and employing organizations can take to support resilience-building. This is divided into resilience-focused interventions (such as resilience workshops) and good management practices that are particularly relevant to developing resilience. Explains the distinction between improving the resilience of individuals and raising levels of well-being in the team ("team resilience").
	■ With reference to the wider contexts of leadership and organizational development and with real-life examples:
	  i. Describe specific ways in which managers and leaders can support resilience development in others
	  ii. Explain how resilience-building can be integrated into leadership development, with reference to some of the most relevant/best known leadership models
	  iii. Illustrate how good management and leadership practices can help build resilience

Chapter 8 ■ Takes an overview of implications for employers, with practical examples of the different forms that team and organizational interventions might take and a guide to using this book to plan your own.	■ Provides a broad overview of key conclusions and principles ■ Sets out a range of practical scenarios for organizational resilience-building interventions, with reference to real-life examples
Appendix II ■ Guidelines on creating a personal resilience plan.	
Appendix III ■ Offers a detailed list of topics that can be included in resilience training and development.	

APPENDIX II

CREATING AN INDIVIDUAL RESILIENCE PLAN

Small steps taken every day will be more effective in building resilience than grand plans that go nowhere. We often set goals that are aspirational and at the time of setting them it eases our conscience and we feel we are doing something in the right direction. More often than not the goals serve only to make us feel guilty. Very often we end up feeling de-moralized and rationalize our inaction in a variety of creative ways.

The three keys to turning goals into action and behavior that makes a real difference are:

1. realistic goal-setting;
2. creating rituals;
3. getting support.

It is well known that goals need to be specific, measurable, achievable, realistic, and timed (the famous SMART acronym), but setting goals is not enough. A commitment to action is required that triggers other action that delivers the sought after benefits.

This is where rituals come in.[1] Rituals turn wishful thinking into regular habits. Small steps taken consistently over a period of time have a much bigger effect than big leaps that are hard to achieve or are intermittent. Sometimes the biggest barrier to achieving a goal is getting started. Activation energy is all that is required to set a process in motion the rituals that catalyze bigger results.

The hardest things about going for a run could be getting your running shoes on. Leave them by the door so that when you get home from work you are immediately reminded of your intention to run regularly and putting them on is the catalyst you need. Shaun Achor gives the example of taking out the batteries of the remote control for his TV.[2] The effort of going to get them (20–30 seconds) is sometimes too much and he does not automatically switch on the TV when he gets home. He says he ends up playing his guitar instead. Building rituals requires defining very precise behaviors and performing them at very specific times, motivated by deeply held commitment to the bigger goal.

Jim Loehr and Tony Schwarz describe six steps for creating and maintaining rituals:

Step 1 Identify the goal, large or small. The goal must be heartfelt and rooted in a deep desire to bring about change.

Step 2 Think of things you can do that are small in themselves but will have a cumulative or contributory effect towards achieving your goal.

Step 3 Share your thinking with others. Get ideas, reactions from other people.

Step 4 Choose specific times in the day or week, same time each time, when you will carry out the small step. Ensure it is precise and specific. Where possible build them into your daily, weekly routines.

Step 5 Where appropriate keep a log or some form of monitoring. Record the effects the ritual is having.

Step 6 Keep them going for at least one to two months until they really start paying off and become habitual, almost automatic behaviors.

Here are some examples of rituals to help you formulate your own. Note the difference between wishful thinking, mantras, and rituals.

Wishful thinking	Mantra (What I want)	My ritual
I must get fitter	I must exercise more	Between 6 and 6.30 pm on Mon, Wed, and Fri I will go for a 30-minute run
I wish I could be an artist	I must paint and draw more	Sunday mornings between 10 am and 1pm is my dedicated painting time
I wish I was not such a slave to email	Manage my email, not the other way round	Check my email only at these times every day; switch off the email alert
I wish I did not bring so much work home	I will limit the amount of work I do at home	I will go online only between 7 pm and 9 pm without exception
I wish I had the time to talk to my friends	I must contact my friends more	The first call I will make from the car at the end of each day will always be to a friend
I wish I could get better sleep	Go to bed at a more regular time	Set the alarm at 10.30 to go to bed by 11pm
I wish my work did not always interrupt my family life in the evenings	More quality time with the family each night	Set my BlackBerry to switch off at 6 pm and come on again at 9 pm to protect my family time

Research studies[3] have shown that people who tend to achieve their goals:

1. Envision themselves having succeeded.
2. Pick moderately challenging goals.
3. Balance optimism with pessimism to achieve a sense of realism (unbridled optimism can lead to failure and depression).
4. Make detailed plans.
5. Monitor progress.
6. Seek help and advice.
7. Enjoy the journey.

Recent advances in neuroscience have given us clues in how to use the way the brain works to increase our focus and attention. Here are a few tips to help you rewire your brain. Will-power is needed to overcome natural resistance of the brain to form new habits. The best way to achieve a strong will is a clear sense of purpose.

Always remind yourself of the following:

What is the objective, the end point?
What benefits are in it for me?
What are the consequences of not changing?
What might I lose out on if I don't change?
What will it feel like when I achieve my goals?
What is the best possible outcome for me?

Secondly, seek to substitute new behaviors rather than try to eliminate the old ones. By substituting new behaviors you are creating and strengthening new neural pathways. Concentrating and paying attention to what you are trying to achieve strengthens the brain's neural connections and pathways.

Successful behavior change requires concerted effort and repetition. One way to help achieve this is by rehearsing the new behavior in your mind. This is a technique known and used by world-class musicians and sports people, as well as actors and politicians. Mental rehearsal uses many of the brain's neural circuits that are required to do it for real.

In addition, it helps to act as if you have already mastered the new behavior or habit. This will stimulate the similar brain circuits and neural transmitters to those involved in doing it for real, just as smiling can help you feel more cheerful even when you are sad. Act like a confident person and you will feel more confident. It also helps to make mental notes as well as physical notes to increase focus and concentration. Bringing about real change in our lives is not easy but it is not that difficult either if you use the right techniques.

Create a target for the next three months under one or more of the main resilience factors:

1. Adaptability;
2. Confidence;
3. Social Support;
4. Purposefulness.

You can also create resilience-building objectives that cover the physical/biological dimensions of exercise, sleep, and nutrition.

Then think about what you need to do and whom to involve. These are your Enablers and can include buying books, watching videos, finding out about local community groups, courses on offer etc. It can include people to talk to, consult, or negotiate with. Think of people whom you can invite to join you for support and also have fun doing it.

Finally, think about rituals that will help you get where you want to go. Your plan will be more powerful if shared with others, especially where they help you and you help them with ideas, support, and encouragement.

Without some form of plan it is unlikely you will be able to bring about the changes you wish to see in your life. Real change requires a clear vision of what you want to achieve, realistic achievable goals, a plan, self-discipline, and effort.

With regard to achieving goals there are three golden rules:

1. Think big, but take small steps.
2. Persistence pays.
3. Involve others in the plan and the progress.

APPENDIX III

CORE TOPICS FOR RESILIENCE-BUILDING

Key components for individual resilience-building can be drawn upon to create training or development resources such as courses, coaching, or leadership development. These components have been described and discussed in Chapters 4 and 5, with the diagnostic frameworks and tools set out in Chapters 1 and 2.

1. Understanding the nature of resilience.
    a. narrow or reactive (heroic) resilience;
    b. routine resilience and the relationship to personality and the situation;
    c. the potential benefits of building resilience
        i. to the individual;
        ii. to the organization;
    d. the two broad approaches, emotions and cognition;
    e. its multi-dimensional and complex nature.
2. Measuring individual resilience.
3. Physical/biological foundations.
    a. amount and intensity of physical activity;
    b. sleep;
    c. healthy diet.
4. The key role played by positive emotions.
    a. how positive emotions differ from negative emotions;
    b. the research on positive emotions and benefits to the individual;
    c. role of gratitude, forgiveness, compassion in particular;
    d. acts of kindness.
    e. the positivity ratio and how to assess it;
    f. learning mindfulness and savoring;
    g. meditating and reflecting.
5. Achieving quality social relationships at work and in life as a whole.
    a. building positive relationships;
    b. turning round difficult relationships;
    c. communicating constructively (including giving feedback);

    d.   identifying and strengthening support networks;

    e.   assertion and courageous conversations.

6. Identifying and using strengths
   a. in yourself;
   b. in others
   c. benefits to individual and the organization of a strengths focus;
   d. assessing strengths;
   e. finding new and different ways for using strengths;
   f. getting into Flow;

7. Developing positive mindsets.
   a. identifying and eliminating automatic negative thoughts;
   b. building optimism;
   c. re-framing;
   d. learning from failure and mistakes;
   e. positive frames of mind, e.g. growth v fixed mindset.

8. Developing coping skills.
   a. problem-solving under pressure;
   b. energy management;
   c. staying calm;

9. Meaning and values.
   a. identifying what is really important to you;
   b. finding meaning in your work and your life as a whole;
   c. job-crafting;
   d. Appreciative Inquiry;
   e. contributing, volunteering, making a difference.

10. Importance of goals.
    a. intrinsically v. extrinsically satisfying goals;
    b. goals linked to core values.

11. Creating realistic plans that will bring about lasting behavior change.
    a. creating a resilience plan;
    b. role of rituals;
    c. need for social support.

NOTES

INTRODUCTION—SETTING THE SCENE

1. Reich, J. W., Zautra, A. J. & Hall, J. S. (eds) (2012) *Handbook of Adult Resilience*, New York, The Guildford Press.
2. Lazarus, R. S. (1994) Individual Differences in Emotion. In P. Ekman & R. J. Davidson (eds), *The Nature of Emotions,* pp. 332–336, New York: Oxford University Press.
3. Palmer, S. & Cooper, C. (2010) *How to Deal with Stress*. London: Kogan Page.
4. Kobasa, Suzanne C. (1979) Stressful Life Events, Personality, and Health: An Inquiry into Hardiness. *Journal of Personality and Social Psychology*, 37(1), January.
5. Proudfoot, J. G., Corr, P. J., Guest, D. E. & Dunn, G. (2009) Cognitive-Behavioural Training to Change Attributional Style Improves Employee Well-Being, Job Satisfaction, Productivity, and Turnover. *Personality and Individual Differences* 46, 147–153.
6. This concept originated in the study of organizational change and development (OD), where it has been defined as "organizational members' shared resolve to implement a change (change commitment) and shared belief in their collective capability to do so (change efficacy)" (Weiner, B. J. (2009), A Theory of Organizational Readiness for Change, *Implementation Science*, 4(1), 67). It has also been applied to learning and development, where it has been shown to be one of the key success factors in world-class leadership development programs (Robertson, I. T., 2004, World Class Leadership Development, Summary Report for the UK Cabinet Office).
7. *The Guardian*, October 21, 2011.
8. Reuters, November 2, 2011.

1 "THE INDIVIDUAL"—A FRAMEWORK FOR UNDERSTANDING PERSONAL RESILIENCE

1. Bonanno, G. A. (2005) Resilience in the Face of Potential Trauma, *Current Directions in Psychological Science*, June, 14(3), 135–138.
2. Reich, J. W., Zautra, A. J., & Hall, J. S. (eds) (2012) *Handbook of Adult Resilience*, New York: The Guildford Press.

3. Rutter, M. (2007) Resilience, Competence, and Coping. *Child Abuse & Neglect*, March, 31(3), 205–209, p. 205.
4. Charney, D. S. (2004) Psychobiological Mechanisms of Resilience and Vulnerability: Implications for Successful Adaptation to Extreme Stress, *Focus*, 2, 368–391, American Psychiatric Association, cited in Reich et al. (2012), p. 35.
5. Tugade, M. M. & Fredrickson, B. L. (2004) Resilient Individuals Use Positive Emotions to Bounce Back From Negative Emotional Experiences, *Journal of Personality and Social Psychology*, 86(2), 320–333, p. 320.
6. Windle, G., Bennett, Kate M., & Noyes, J. (2011) A Methodological Review of Resilience Measurement Scales, *Health and Quality of Life Outcomes*, 9(8), 1–18.
7. Peterson, C. & Seligman, M. E. P. (2004) *Character Strengths and Virtues*, New York: Oxford University Press.
8. Masten, A. S. & Wright, M.O'D (2010) Resilience over the Lifespan: Developmental Perspectives on Resistance, Recovery, and Transformation, cited in Reich et al. (2012), pp. 213–237.
9. Gallo, L. C. & Matthews, K. A. (2003) Understanding the Association between Socioeconomic Status and Physical Health: Do Negative Emotions Play a Role? *Psychological Bulletin*, 129, 10–51.
10. Peterson & Seligman, (2004) p. 78.
11. Johnson, S. (2009) Organizational Screening: The ASSET Model. In S. Cartwright and C. L. Cooper (eds) *Oxford Handbook on Organizational Well-being*, pp. 133-155, Oxford: Oxford University Press.
12. Coutu, D. L. (2003) How Resilience Works. In *Harvard Business Review on Building Personal and Organizational Resilience*, Boston: Harvard Business School Publishing Corporation.
13. Maddi & Khoshaba (2005).
14. Charney, D. S. (2004) Psychobiological Mechanisms of Resilience and Vulnerability: Implications for Successful Adaptation to Extreme Stress, *Focus*, 2, 368–391, American Psychiatric Association.
15. Smith, T. W. (2006) Personality as Risk and Resilience in Physical Health, *Current Directions in Psychological Science*, October, 15(5), 227–231.
16. Mancini, A. D. & Bonnano, G. A. (2009) *Journal of Personality Special Issue*: Resilience in Common Life: Resources, Mechanisms, and Interventions: Ed. Davis, M. C., Luecken, L., & Lemery-Chalfant, K., December, 77(6), 1637–1644.
17. Skodol, A. E. (2010) The Resilient Personality. In Reich et al. (2012), pp. 112–125.
18. Costa, P. T., Jr. & McCrae, R. R. (1992) Revised NEO Personality Inventory (NEO-PI-R) and NEO Five-Factor Inventory (NEO-FFI) manual. Odessa, FL: Psychological Assessment Resources.
19. Mayer, J. D. & Faber, M. A. (2010) Personal Intelligence and Resilience: Recovery in the Shadow of Broken Connections. In Reich et al. (2012), pp. 94–111.
20. Poropat, A. E. (2009) A Meta-Analysis of the Five-Factor Model of Personality and Academic Performance. *Psychological Bulletin*, 135(2), 322–338.

21. Flint-Taylor, J. & Robertson, I. T. (2007) Leader Personality and Workforce Performance: The Role of Psychological Well-Being. EAWOP 2007 (XIIIth European Congress of Work and Organizational Psychology), Stockholm.
22. Barrick, M. R., & Mount, M. K. (1991) The Big Five Personality Dimensions and Job Performance: a Meta-Analysis, *Personnel Psychology*, 44, 1–26.
23. Tett, R. P., Jackson, D. N., & Rothstein, M. (1991) Personality Measures as Predictors of Job Performance: a Meta-Analytic Review. *Personnel Psychology*, 44, 703–742.
24. Cattell, R. B. (1973) *Personality and Mood by Questionnaire*, San Francisco: Jossey-Bass.
25. Myers, I. B. with Peter B. Myers (1980, 1995) *Gifts Differing: Understanding Personality Type*, Mountain View, CA: Davies-Black Publishing.
26. Saville, P., Holdsworth, R., Nyfield, G., Cramp, L. & Mabey, W. (1984) The Occupational Personality Questionnaire (OPQ), SHL: London.
27. Flint-Taylor, J. and Robertson, I. T. (2007) Leaders' Impact on Well-Being and Performance. British Psychological Society Division of Occupational Psychology Annual Conference.
28. Kobasa, Suzanne C. (1979) Stressful Life Events, Personality, and Health: An Inquiry into Hardiness. *Journal of Personality and Social Psychology*, January, 37(1), 1–11.
29. Maddi, S. R. & Khoshaba, D. M. (2005) *Resilience at Work: How to Succeed No Matter What Life Throws at You*, New York: Amacom.
30. Nicholls, A. R., Polman, R. C. J., Levy, A. R. & Backhouse, S .H. (2008) Mental Toughness, Optimism, Pessimism, and Coping Among Athletes, *Personality and Individual Differences*, April, 44(5), 1182–1192.
31. Clough, P. J., Earle, K. & Sewell, D. F. (2002) Mental Toughness: The Concept and Its Measurement. In I. Cockerill (ed.) *Solutions in Sport Psychology*, pp. 32–47, Thompson: London.
32. Nicholls et al., 2008.
33. Masten, A. S. & Wright, M.O'D (2010) Resilience over the Lifespan: Developmental Perspectives on Resistance, Recovery, and Transformation. In Reich et al. (2012), pp. 213–237.
34. Boyatzis, R. E., Goleman, D., & Rhee, K. S. (2000) Clustering Competence in Emotional Intelligence. In Bar-On, Reuven & Parker, James D. A.(ed.) *The Handbook of Emotional Intelligence: Theory, Development, Assessment, and Application at Home, School, and in the Workplace*, San Francisco, CA: Jossey-Bass.
35. Flint-Taylor, J., Robertson, I., & Gray, J. (1999) The Five-Factor Model of Personality: Levels of Measurement and the Prediction of Managerial Performance and Attitudes. British Psychological Society Occupational Psychology Conference.
36. Tugade & Fredrickson (2004).
37. Fredrickson, B. L., Tugade, M. M., Waugh, C. E., & Larkin, G. R. (2003) What Good Are Positive Emotions in Crises? a Prospective Study of Resilience and Emotions Following the Terrorist Attacks on the United States on September 11th, 2001, *Journal of Personality and Social Psychology*, 84(2), 365–376.

38. Ellis, A. (1991) The Revised ABC's of Rational-Emotive Therapy (RET), *Journal of Rational-Emotive & Cognitive-Behaviour Therapy*, 9(3), 139–172.
39. Seligman, Martin E. P. (1991) *Learned Optimism: How to Change Your Mind and Your Life*, New York: Knopf.
40. Marshall, G. N., Wortman, C. B., Kusulas, J. W., Hervig, L. K., Vickers Jr., R. R. (1992) Distinguishing Optimism from Pessimism: Relations to Fundamental Dimensions of Mood and Personality, *Journal of Personality and Social Psychology*, 62(6), 1067–1074.
41. Costa, P. T., Jr., McCrae, R. R., & Dye, D. A. (1991) Facet Scales for Agreeableness and Conscientiousness: a Revision of the neo Personality Inventory. *Personality and Individual Differences*, 12, 887–898.
42. Frankl, V. E. (1959). *Man's Search for Meaning: An Introduction to Logotherapy*. New York: Simon & Schuster.
43. Tugade & Fredrickson (2004).
44. Parkes, K. R. and Rendell, D. (1988) The Hardy Personality and Its Relationship to Extraversion and Neuroticism, *Personality and Individual Differences*, 9(4), 785–790; Maddi, S. R., Khoshaba, D. M., Persico, M., Lu, J., Harvey, R., & Bleecker, F. (2002), The Personality Construct of Hardiness: Relationships with Comprehensive Tests of Personality and Psychopathology, *Journal of Research in Personality*, 36(1), 72–85; Horsburgh, V., Schermer, J., Veselka, L., & Vernon, P. (2009) a Behavioural Genetic Study of Mental Toughness and Personality. *Personality and Individual Differences*, 46(2), 100–105.
45. www.robertsoncooper.com
46. Flint-Taylor, J. & Robertson, I.T. (2013) Enhancing well-being in organizations through selection and development. In R.J. Burke & C.L. Cooper (eds), *The Fulfilling Workplace*, pp. 165–186, Farnham: Gower.
47. Windle et al. (2011), 17.
48. Block, J. & Kremen, A. M. (1996) IQ and Ego-Resiliency: Conceptual and Empirical Connections and Separateness, *Journal of Personality and Social Psychology*, 70, 349–361; Klohnen, E. C. (1996) Conceptual Analysis and Measurement of the Construct of Ego-Resiliency, *Journal of Personality and Social Psychology*, 70, 1067–1079.
49. Peterson, C., Semmel, A., von Baeyer, C., Abramson, L. Y., Metalsky, G. I., and Seligman, Martin E. P. (1982) The Attributional Style Questionnaire, *Cognitive Therapy and Research*, 6(3), 287–299.

2 "THE INDIVIDUAL + THE SITUATION"—PERSONAL RESILIENCE AT WORK

1. Johnson, S. (2009). Organizational Screening: The ASSET Model. In S. Cartwright and C. L. Cooper (eds) *Oxford Handbook on Organizational Well-being*. Oxford: Oxford University Press.
2. Besag, V. E. (1989). *Bullies and Victims in Schools*. Milton Keynes, England: Open University Press.

3. Safian, R. (2012). This Is Generation Flux: Meet the Pioneers of the New (and Chaotic) Frontier of Business. *Fast Company*, January 9.
4. McClelland, D. C. (1998). Identifying Competencies with Behavioral-Event Interviews, *Psychological Science* 9(5), 331–339.
5. Goleman, D. (1998). *Working with Emotional Intelligence*. New York: Bantam Books.
6. McClelland, D. D. (1973). Testing for Competence Rather Than for "Intelligence." *American Psychologist*, 28(1), 1–14.

3 RESILIENCE-BUILDING OVER THE YEARS—FROM REMEDIAL TO PERFORMANCE-ENHANCING

1. Proudfoot, J., Guest, D., Carson, J., Dunn, G., & Gray, J. (1997) Effect of Cognitive-Behavioural Training on Job-Finding Among Long-Term Unemployed People. *The Lancet*, 350(9071), 96–100.
2. Rose V., Harris E. (2004) From Efficacy to Effectiveness: Case Studies in Unemployment Research. *Journal of Public Health* (Oxford), 26, 297–302.
3. Collard, B., Epperheimer, J. W., & Saign, D. (1996) Career Resilience in a Changing Workplace, Columbus, Ohio, ERIC Clearinghouse on Adult, Career, and Vocational Education.
4. Waterman, R.H., Waterman, J.A., Collard, B.A. (1994) Toward a Career-Resilient Workforce, *Harvard Business Review*, 72(4), July/August, 87–95.
5. Ibid.
6. GlaxoSmithKline – Stress Management, Health, Work and Well-Being Case Studies, Department for Work and Pensions, http://www.dwp.gov.uk/health-work-and-well-being/case-studies/gsk-stress/
7. Robertson, I. & Cooper, C. (2011) *Well-Being, Productivity and Happiness at Work*, Basingstoke: Palgrave Macmillan, p. 128.
8. Cooper, C. L. & Cartwright, S. (1997) An Intervention Strategy for Workplace Stress, *Journal of Psychosomatic Research* 43(1), 7–16.
9. Cooper, C. & Finkelstein, S. (2012) *Advances in Mergers & Acquisitions*, Bingley: Emerald.
10. van der Klink, J. J., Blonk, R., Schene, A. H., & van Dijk, F. J. H. (2001) The Benefits of Interventions for Work-Related Stress. *American Journal of Public Health*, 91, 270–276.
11. Jordan, J., Gurr, E., Tinline, G., Giga, S. I., Faragher, B., & Cooper, C. L. (2003) *Beacons of Excellence in Stress Prevention*: Research Report 133. London, U.K.: UK Health and Safety Executive Books, p. 194.
12. Cartwright, S. & Cooper, C. (2011) *Innovation in Stress and Health*, Basingstoke: Palgrave Macmillan.
13. Cooper, C., Goswami, U., & Sahakian, B. J. (2009) *Mental Capital and Wellbeing*, Oxford: Wiley-Blackwell.
14. MacLeod, D. & Clarke, N. (2009) *Engaging for Success: Enhancing Performance through Employee Engagement*. London: Department for Business, Innovation and Skills (BIS), p. 9.

15. Robertson & Cooper, *Well-Being*, p. 138.
16. Donald, I., Taylor, P., Johnson, S., Cooper, C. L., Cartwright, S., & Robertson, S. (2005) Work Environments, Stress and Productivity: An Examination Using *ASSET*. *International Journal of Stress Management*, 12(4), 409–423.
17. Cropanzano, R., & Wright, T. A. (1999) A Five-Year Study of the Relationship between Well-Being and Performance. *Journal of Consulting Psychology*, 51, 252–265.
18. Harter, J. K., Schmidt, F. L., & Keyes, C. L. M. (2003) Well-Being in the Workplace and Its Relationship to Business Outcomes: a Review of the Gallup Studies. In C. L. M. Keyes & J. Haidt (eds), *Flourishing: Positive Psychology and the Life Well-Lived* (pp. 205–224), Washington, DC: American Psychological Association.
19. Luthans, F., Luthans, K., & Luthans, B. (2004) Positive Psychological Capital: Going beyond Human and Social Capital, *Business Horizons*, 47(1), 45–50.
20. Positive Psychology Center website, ppc.sas.upenn.edu, University of Pennsylvania, 2007.
21. Staal, M. A. (2004) Stress, Cognition, and Human Performance: A Literature Review and Conceptual Framework, NASA, Moffet Field, CA.
22. Lundberg, U. & Cooper, C. (2010) *The Science of Occupational Health*, Oxford: Wiley-Blackwell.
23. Dollard, M. F., Winefield, H. R., Winefield, A. H. & de Jonge, J. (2000), Psychosocial Job Strain and Productivity in Human Service Workers: a Test of the Demand-Control-Support Model, *Journal of Occupational and Organizational Psychology*, 73, 501–510.
24. LePine, J. A. Podsakoff, N. P. & LePine, M. A. (2005) A Meta-Analytic Test of the Challenge Stressor-Hindrance Stressor Framework: An Explanation for Inconsistent Relationships Among Stressors and Performance. *Academy of Management Journal*, 48, 764–775.
25. Braskamp, L. A., & Wergin, J. F. (2008). Inside-out leadership. Liberal Learning, Association of American Colleges and Universities, 30–35.
26. Flint-Taylor, J. & Robertson, I. T. (2007) Leader Personality and Workforce Performance: The Role of Psychological Well-Being. EAWOP 2007 (XIIIth European Congress of Work and Organizational Psychology), Stockholm; Flint-Taylor, J. & Robertson, I.T. (2007) Leaders' Impact on Well-Being and Performance. British Psychological Society Division of Occupational Psychology Annual Conference.
27. Flint-Taylor, J. (2008) Too Much of a Good Thing? Leadership Strengths as Risks to Well-Being and Performance in the Team. British Psychological Society Division of Occupational Psychology Annual Conference; Kaplan, B. & Kaiser, R. (2006). *The Versatile Leader: Make the Most of Your Strengths—without Overdoing It.* San Francisco, CA: Pfeiffer.

4 WHAT INDIVIDUALS CAN DO TO BUILD THEIR RESILIENCE

1. Five-Factor (FFM) personality questionnaire with a report that looks directly at strengths and risks in relation to the four main components of resilience and the six workplace sources of pressure and support.

2. This is described in Richard Layard's (2005) excellent book, *Happiness: Lessons From a New Science*, Penguin Books.

3. In 2005 Sonja Lyubomirsky, Laura King and Ed Diener published the results of a massive analysis of 225 separate scientific studies on happiness, some of which tracked the same people over long periods of time. This research is described by Sonja Lyubomirsky (2007) in her book *The How of Happiness*.

4. *Learned Optimism* by Martin Seligman (1997) describes groundbreaking research with tried and tested self-assessments and practical exercises that help you move from a pessimistic to a more optimistic outlook with proven benefits in lowered anxiety, improved immune system, increased personal potential, and well-being. His more recent book *Flourish* (2010) contains a useful update of all the possible benefits from an optimistic outlook, and how it can be learned.

5. This is a well-researched and practical book on the power of Mindset (the growth v a fixed mindset in particular). *Mindset: The New Psychology of Success* by Carol Dweck (2007), Random House.

6. Go to http://www.authentichappiness.sas.upenn.edu and complete the Optimism Test.

7. From *Solving Life's Problems* (2007) by Nezu, A., Nezu, C. and D'Zurilla. Springer, New York.

8. Steven Thomson, The Benefits of Merit-Finding. *Psychology Today* (1985).

9. The best book on this subject is *The Resilience Factor: Seven Keys to Finding Your Inner Strength and Overcoming Life's Hurdles* by Karen Reivich and Andrew Shatte (2002), Broadway Books.

10. Figures quoted by Tal Ben-Shahar in his wildly popular series of lectures on happiness and positive psychology delivered at Harvard University in 2003.

11. Positivity by Barbara Fredrickson (2008) is a groundbreaking book based on exhaustive research that led to the notion that positive emotions make us more effective in the present and also build our resources for the future. She also identified the critical Positivity/negativity Ratio.

12. Kim Cameron at the University of Michigan is a leading light in this new area of research. http://www.centerforpos.org/

13. A good book on this subject is *Human Natures: Genes, Cultures and the Human Prospect* by Paul R. Ehrlich (2000), Island Press.

14. For a detailed description of the Barbara Fredrickson's *Strengthen and Build Theory of Positive Emotions* and to see the latest research go to http://www.unc.edu/peplab/broaden_build.html

15. If you want to know your ratio go to www.positivityratio.com, and complete the Positivity Test (© Dr Barbara Fredrickson 2009).

5 WHAT INDIVIDUALS CAN DO: STRENGTHENING THE FOUR PERSONAL RESILIENCE RESOURCES

1. From Average to A+ by Alex Linley (2008) CAPP Press, UK. The list of questions is reproduced with permission of The Centre for Applied Positive Psychology.

2. See for example Buckingham, M. & Clifton, D. (2001) *Now Discover Your Strengths*. The Free Press, New York. See also Linley, A. (2010) *The Strengths Book*, CAPP Press, UK.

3. Peterson, C. & Seligman, M. (2004) *Character Strengths and Virtues: A Handbook and Classification*. New York: Oxford University Press; Washington, DC: American Psychological Association.

4. For the latest research go to www.viastrengths.org /www/en-us/research/summaries.aspx

5. Go to http://www.authentichappiness.sas.upenn.edu

6. http://www.cappeu.com/Realise2.aspx

7. Linley, A., Willars, J. & Biswas-Diener, R. (2010) *The Strengths Book: Be Confident, Be Successful, and Enjoy Better Relationships by Realising the Best of You*, CAPP Press.

8. Rath, T. & Conchie, B. (2008) *Strengths-Based Leadership*, Gallup Press gives access to StrengthsFinder the online strenghs assessment based on Gallup research.

9. Go to www.strengths.gallup.com

10. The classic work is *Flow: The Psychology of Optimal Experience* by Mihaly Csikszentmihalyi (1990), who was the originator of the idea and is most strongly associated with ongoing research on Flow. See also his book *Finding Flow: The Psychology of Engagement in Everyday Life* (2007).

11. Gardner, H. (2nd edn, 1993) *Frames of Mind: The Theory of Multiple Intelligences*, London: HarperCollins.

12. Zimbardo, P. & Boyd, J. (2008) *The Time Paradox: The New Psychology of Tie that Will Change your Life*, New York: Free Press.

13. See Jane Dutton's work at the University of Michigan http://www.bus.umich.edu/facultybios/facultybio.asp?id=000119663 and also The Compassion Lab at http://www.compassionlab.org/teaching.htm

14. Gable, S. L. et al. (2004) What Do You Do when Things Go Right? The Intrapersonal and Interpersonal Benefits of Sharing Positive Events. *Journal of Personality and Social Psychology*, 87, 228–245.

15. For more on the research on the benefits of social relationships go to http://diener.socialpsychology.org/

16. See Nature Neuroscience, tinyurl.com/28rgcwm

17. Maisel, N. & Gable, S. L. (2009) The Paradox of Received Social Support: the Importance of Responsiveness. *Psychological Science*, 20, 928–932.

18. For the research on gratitude see Emmons, R. (2007) *Thanks! How the New Science of Gratitude Can Make you Happier*, University of California, Davis.

19. http://www.apple.com/itunes/

20. Palmer, S. & Cooper, C. (3rd edn, 2012) *How to Deal with Stress*, London: Kogan Page.

21. See Kotter, J. P. (1995) Leading Change: Why Transformation Efforts Fail. *Harvard Business Review*, 73(2), 59–63.

22. Charney, D. & Nemeroff, C. (2004) *The Peace of Mind Prescription: An Authoritative Guide to Finding the Most Effective Treatment for Anxiety and Depression*, New York: Houghton Mifflin.

23. Medina, J. (2009) *Brain Rules* is a general guide to the brain, and is particularly helpful on physical exercise, sleep, stress and also learning.
24. Seligman, M. (2011) *Flourish*, New York: Free Press.
25. Go to http://www.topendsports.com/testing/index.htm to see a range of fitness tests to choose from
26. The US Department of health National Activity Guidelines can be found at http://www.health.gov/paguidelines/ The site also summarizes the dramatic research findings on the relationship between lack of activity and ill-health
27. Two apps that the authors have personal experience with are http://www.fitbit.com/ which uses Wi-Fi communication devices and mobile apps, and http://www.rallyon.com/ which is organizationally orientated for workplace wellness programs.
28. Go to The Sleep Well at http://www.stanford.edu/~dement/
29. The latest US Official guidelines on healthy eating are at http://www.health.gov/dietaryguidelines/2010.asp
30. Southwick, S. M. & Charney, D. S. (2012) *Resilience: The Science of Mastering Life's Greatest Challenges*, Cambridge: Cambridge University Press.
31. The philosopher Daniel Dennnet is very good on this subject (see his 2006 book *Breaking the Spell: Religion as Natural Phenomenon*). See also Haidt, J. (2012), *The Righteous Mind: Why Good People are Divided by Politics and Religion*.
32. Valliant, G. (2008) *Spiritual Evolution: A Scientific Defence of Faith* is an in-depth integration of neuro-science, evolutionary biology, positive psychology and the issue human spirituality
33. http://eu.pfeiffer.com/WileyCDA/Section/id-811595.html
34. Detailed guidance from the researchers on turning your job into a calling is at www.bus.umich.edu/Positive/POS-Teaching-and-Learning/Job_Crafting-Theory_to_Practice-Aug_08.pdf
35. Two of the foremost researchers on Goal Setting are Robert Emmons at UC Davis and Ken Sheldon at the University of Missouri. A review of the scientific evidence showing that pursuing materialistic (i.e. extrinsically satisfying) goals and desires can be harmful to well-being can be found in Kasser, T. (2002) Sketches for a Self-Determination Theory of Values. In E. L. Deci & R. M. Ryan (Eds.), *Handbook of Self-Determination Research* (pp. 123–140). Rochester, NY: University Of Rochester Press.
36. Perhaps one of the best books on this subject is the very influential *From Good To Great* by Jim Collins and Porras (2001) published by HarperCollins, New York.
37. One way to discover what is important to the individual is to complete the VIA Strengths Survey described earlier in this chapter. Signature strengths will tend to cluster around one or more of the six universal values. In addition, the Personal Values Survey is at http://www.intentionalhappiness.com.
38. See Schmuck, P. & Sheldon, K. (2001) *Lifegoals and Well-being: Toward a Positive Psychology of Human Striving*. This is a collection of research

articles showing the link between goals and life satisfaction, with an emphasis on those goals that most likely promote happiness.

39. For detailed descriptions of mindfulness and meditation techniques, see books and CDs by Jon Kabat-Zinn. For example, *Calming Your Anxious Mind* (2009). Mindfulness meditation techniques can also be very powerful as aids to stress reduction and pain management.

40. Bryant, E. & Veroff, J. (2007) *Savoring: A New Model of Positive Experience* is a comprehensive review of research that shows that it is possible to savor past experiences by recalling them positively, enjoying present activities as they happen, and planning to savor future moments by anticipating them.

6 ORGANIZATIONAL APPROACHES: THE INDIVIDUAL AT WORK

1. See Charney, D. & Nemeroff, C. (2004) *The Peace of Mind Prescription*, New York: Houghton Mifflin.
2. For more on Wave Professional Styles Questionnaire go to http://www.savilleconsulting.com/index.aspx
3. Robertson I. T. & Flint-Taylor, J. (2009) Leadership, Psychological Well-Being and Organizational Outcomes. In S. Cartwright & C. L. Cooper (eds), *Oxford Handbook on Organizational Well-being*, Oxford: Oxford University Press.
4. Robertson Cooper Ltd. http://www.robertsoncooper.com/
5. http://www.hoganassessments.com/
6. The HDS scales are reproduced with permission of Hogan Assessments, Tulsa, Oklahoma, USA.
7. Sutton, R. (2010) *The No Asshole Rule: Building a Civilized Workplace and Surviving One That Isn't*, New York: Business Plus.
8. Myers, I. B. & Myers, P. B. (1980) *Gifts Differing: Understanding Personality Type*, Mountain View, CA: Consulting Psychologists Press.
9. Ibid.
10. Hirsh, S. K. & Kummerov, J. M. (3rd edn. 2000) *Introduction to Type in Organizations*, Oxford: Oxford Psychologists Press.
11. Kaplan, B., & Kaiser, R. (2006) *The Versatile Leader: Make the Most of Your Strengths—without Overdoing It*, San Francisco: Pfeiffer.
12. www.towerswatson.com/services/employees-surveys
13. www.robertsoncooper.com/iresilience/
14. http://www.ashridge.org.uk/website/content.nsf/wELNPSY/Psychometrics:+Ashridge?opendocument
15. http://www.haygroup.com/ In addition to online resilience assessments Hay Group also offer a Resilience Workbook at http://www.haygroup.com/leadershipandtalentondemand/ourproducts/item_details.aspx?itemid=117&type=1
16. The seven skills to boost resilience are reproduced with permission from Hay Group.
16. http://www.hardinessinstitute.com/

17. Maddi, S. R. & Khoshaba, D. M. (2005) *Resilience at Work: How to Succeed No Matter What Life Throws at You*, New York: AMACOM.
18. Loehr, J. & Schwartz, T. (2005) *The Power of Full Engagement*, New York: Free Press.

7 ORGANIZATIONAL INTERVENTIONS: THE WORKPLACE SITUATION

1. Fredrickson, B. & Losada, M. (2005) Positive Emotions and the Complex Dynamics of Human Flourishing. *American Psychologist*, 60, 678–686.
2. Rath, T. & Harter, J. (2010) *The Economics of Wellbeing*. New York: The Gallup Organization.
3. http://www.bus.umich.edu/Positive/POS-Teaching-and-Learning/Job_Crafting-Theory_to_Practice-Aug_08.pdf
4. http://www.centerforpos.org/the-center/teaching-and-practice-materials/teaching-tools/job-crafting-exercise/
5. Cooperrider, D. L. & Sekerka, L. E. (2003) Elevation of Enquiry into the Appreciable World: Toward a Theory of Positive Organizational Change. In Cameron, K., Dutton, J., & Quin, R. (eds) *Positive Organizational Scholarship*, San Francisco: Berrett-Kohler.
6. Whitney, D., & Trosten-Bloom, A. (2003) *The Power of Appreciative Inquiry: A Practical Guide to Positive Change*, San Francisco: Berrett-Kohler.
7. Rath, T. & Conchie, B. (2008) *Strengths-Based Leadership*, New York: Gallup Press; Buckingham, M. (2007) *Go Put Your Strengths to Work*, New York: Free press.
8. http://www.cappeu.com/
9. The list of business benefits to organizations of a strengths-based approach to managing people is reproduced with permission of the Center for Applied Positive Psychology, Warwick, UK.
10. People born between 1980 and 2000 (approximately), also known as "Generation Y."
11. Meister, J. & Willyerd, K. (2010) *The 2020 Workplace: How Innovative Companies Attract, Develop, and Keep Tomorrow's Employees Today*, New York: HarperCollins.
12. Stavros, J. M. & Wooten, L. (2012) Creating and Sustaining Strengths-Based Strategy That soars and Performs. In Cameron, K. & Spreitzer, G. (eds) *The Oxford Handbook of Positive Organizational Scholarship*, Oxford: Oxford University Press.
13. Kouzes, J. M. & Posner, B. (4th edn, 2007) *The Leadership Challenge*, San Francisco: Wiley.
14. More at http://www.leadershipchallenge.com/
15. Bass, B. & Riggio, R. (2005) *Transformational Leadership*, New Jersey: Laurence Erlbaum Associates.
16. George, B. (2004) *Authentic Leadership: Rediscovering the Secrets to Creating Lasting Value*, San Francisco: Jossey-Bass.

17. Cameron, K. (2008) *Positive Leadership: Strategies for Extraordinary Performance*, San Francisco: Berrett-Kohler.
18. For the reflected best self exercise go to http://www.centerforpos.org/the-center/teaching-and-practice-materials/teaching-tools/reflected-best-self-exercise/
19. See the far-reaching and thorough research described by Richard Kilburg in his book *Virtuous Leaders: Strategy, Character and Influence in the 21st Century* (2012) American Psychological Association.
20. From Comprehensive Soldier Fitness: a Vision for Psychological Resilience in the U.S. Army. *American Psychologist*, (2011), 66(1), 1–3.
21. Seligman, M. (2011) *Flourish: A Visionary New Understanding of Happiness and Well-Being*. New York: Free Press.
22. Reivich, K. Seligman, M. and McBride, S. (2011) Master Resilience Training in the US Army, *American Psychologist*, 66, 1, 25–34.
23. Source:http://www.army.mil/article/72431/Study_concludes_Master_Resilience_Training_effective

8 RESILIENCE-BUILDING: IMPLICATIONS FOR EMPLOYERS

1. For a comprehensive review of international and cultural differences well-being, see Diener, E., Helliwell, J. F. & Kahneman, D. (eds) (2010) *International Differences in Well-Being*, Oxford: Oxford University Press.
2. Overviews of the CSF program are available and regularly updated at www.army.mil/article/72341 and at the University of Pennsylvania Center for Positive Psychology website: www.authentichappiness.sas.upenn.edu/newsletter.aspx?id=1552
3. The US Army's dedicated website for the Comprehensive Soldier Fitness Program is at http://csf.army.mil/faq.html
4. Casey, J. R. (2011) Comprehensive Soldier Fitness: a Vision for Psychological Resilience in the U.S. Army. *American Psychologist*, 66(1), 1–3.
5. They were originally known as War Office Officer Selection Boards.
6. Martin Seligman's April 2011 Harvard Business Review article in which he describes the development of the CSF program is at www.hbr.org/2011/04/building-resilience/ar/pr

APPENDIX 2 CREATING AN INDIVIDUAL RESILIENCE PLAN

1. For more on rituals see Loehr, J. & Schwartz, T. (2004) *The Power of Full Engagement: Managing Energy, Not Time, Is the Key to High Performance and Personal Renewal*, New York: Free Press.
2. Achor, S. (2010) *The Happiness Advantage: The Seven Principles of Positive Psychology That Fuel Success and Performance at Work*, New York: Crown.
3. For more on the research and theory of goals, see Moskowitz, G. B., & Grant, H. (2008) *The Psychology of Goals*, New York: Guilford.

INDEX

Printed and bound by CPI Group (UK) Ltd, Croydon, CR0 4YY